Justice Matters

Essays from the pandemic

Justice Alliance are a collective of organisations and individuals campaigning on issues of access to justice.

The Legal Action Group is a national, independent charity which campaigns for equal access to justice for all members of society. Legal Action Group:

- provides support to the practice of lawyers and advisers
- inspires developments in that practice
- campaigns for improvements in the law and the administration of justice
- stimulates debate on how services should be delivered.

Justice Matters

Essays from the pandemic

Edited for Justice Alliance by
Jessie Brennan, Mandy Groves,
Rhona Friedman, Sue James and
Simon Mullings

 Legal Action Group
2020

Published in Great Britain 2020
by LAG Education and Service Trust Limited
c/o Royalty Studios
105-109 Lancaster Road
London W11 1QF
www.lag.org.uk

British Library Cataloguing in Publication Data

a CIP catalogue record for this book is available from the British Library.
Crown copyright material is produced with the permission of the Controller of
HMSO and the Queen's Printer for Scotland.

This book has been produced using Forest Stewardship
Council (FSC) certified paper. The wood used to produce FSC
certified products with a 'Mixed Sources' label comes from
FSC certified well-managed forests, controlled sources and/or
recycled materials.

Print ISBN: 978 1 913648 05 3
eBook ISBN 978 1 913648 06 0

Typeset by Refinecatch Limited, Bungay, Suffolk
Printed by Hobbs the Printers, Totton, Hampshire

Foreword

Philip Alston, John Norton Pomeroy professor of law at
New York University School of Law and former
United Nations special rapporteur on extreme
poverty and human rights (2014–2020)

This stimulating and insightful collection of essays on the future of
justice in the United Kingdom gives powerful testimony to the fact
that we are living in a time of turmoil and upheaval. The oddity is
that we are doing it in a setting that is seen to be manageable and
potentially orderly and where business-as-usual attitudes still prevail
in many respects. Indeed, perhaps for most of us, the temptation is
to long for a return to the *status quo ante*. But the problem in the UK
is *ante* what exactly? Is it the time when too many of us assumed that
pandemics were a relic of the past, or the days before the upheaval of
the interminable Brexit debates, or the days before the great recession
of 2007 and the subsequent embrace of austerity?

The contributors to this book succeed very well in bringing us
face to face with the devastating consequences not just of COVID-19,
especially for minorities and the least well-off, but of concerted
earlier attempts to reform the justice system. The staggering cuts
to legal aid, the endless pressures on under-resourced courts, and
the introduction of various technologies designed to transform the
system. And looming over all of the challenges identified by the
various authors is the certain prospect of a new set of policies that
will not be called 'austerity version 2.0', but will nevertheless look
all too like the radical policies championed by George Osborne and
David Cameron starting in 2010.

There will be a great many reasons adduced to justify these
policies. They include making up for the medium-term damage to
the economy wrought by the pandemic, the need to pay for the deficit
spending that cushioned economic and social disruption after March

2020, the need to adjust to the long-predicted economic fallout from Brexit, and the need for a new competitiveness to make up for the loss of the stability provided by EU membership.

There is no doubting that new policies are needed to reinvigorate the rule of law and as Baroness Hale puts it, to 'get back to a properly functioning constitution'. At the same time, there will also be an economic crunch generated by all of the challenges listed above, and further compounded by the need for more serious and concerted responses to climate change.

This combination of challenges cannot be met by wanting to return to any particular *status quo ante*. As Lord Beveridge famously noted in 1942, a 'revolutionary moment in the world's history is a time for revolutions, not for patching'. I argued in my 2019 report to the United Nations on poverty in the United Kingdom that austerity version 1.0 was driven not by economic imperatives but by an ideological agenda designed to promote basic neoliberal values and to move definitively away from the assumptions underpinning the notion of a welfare state.

The response to the challenges identified in this book cannot be a piecemeal one, and it should not be conceived of as sector-specific. What is required is a fundamental rethinking of the basic values of the society combined with innovative and creative thinking about how to restructure the economy as a whole to enable it to meet those goals. There is all too little reason to think that this is the direction in which the current government of the UK is heading, but that only makes it all the more important for the lawyers and others whose deep concerns for the future are reflected in this volume to be part of efforts to come up with new and more far-reaching proposals. Legal scholars and law students need to re-imagine the building blocks for training the next generation of lawyers to do much more than uphold existing privilege. And legal practitioners and judges need to ask themselves how best the justice system can be re-oriented to respond not to the issues that pre-occupied us in previous decades but to a world beset by ever-increasing inequality, disastrous levels of global warming, and the continuing marginalisation of the less advantaged in our society.

Philip G Alston
September 2020

Preface

We are living through an unprecedented public health crisis. This book seeks to document, in some small way, the effects of the pandemic viewed through the lens of the justice system. It is a collection of essays which together tell a powerful story of the impact of COVID-19, the responses to it, and the hope for change.

As the pandemic gathered pace, we started to see much more clearly that those in food poverty, from BAME backgrounds, in poor housing, insecure employment, the homeless, the elderly and the disabled were the worst affected. The virus exposed the underlying structural health, race and class inequality in British society. We saw that a decade of austerity had eviscerated health and social care and public services and plunged the justice system into crisis.

But we also saw hope and what can be achieved if there is collective action and the political will. The homeless were housed and those seeking asylum were released from immigration detention. There was a stay on possession cases and a moratorium on benefit sanctions. Ordinary people looked out for each other in ways that we would not previously have imagined. We have worked together and shown what is possible through campaigning, community activism and public pressure, as well as legal challenges. The pandemic presents an opportunity for social justice lawyers to catch the attention of the public, a chance to tell the stories we witness every day and to create solutions that help to build a more just and equal society.

We are grateful to the contributors who have given their time to write about what they have seen and the effects on the clients they represent. Since these essays were commissioned in June 2020, there will have been changes in various areas of the law, just as there has been change with the pandemic itself. Justice Matters is not intended as an end in itself but as the beginning – as a component of a larger discussion about the future, about equality and about justice.

Justice Alliance
September 2020

Contents

Fiona Bawdon | I'm 100% sure statistics alone won't win the battle over legal aid

Why is it that politicians can get away with peddling myths about legal aid fat cats and lies about real cats being given the right to family life by the Human Rights Act?

It's not a new question, but it's one that has been given new urgency by the pandemic.

Much of the answer lies in the power of storytelling. What populist politicians and all tabloid newspaper editors instinctively understand is that telling the best story is the easiest way to win an argument or trounce the opposition – particularly if your opponent is earnestly relying on detailed facts and statistics to make their case. (As everyone knows, statistics are in the same category as lies and damned lies – and anyway 72.5% of them are made up.)

Guardian columnist Jonathan Freedland says: 'The political brain is an emotional brain. It responds not to data, but to instinct and feeling.' It's a lesson that not just legal aid lawyers (and their representative groups) but progressives of all stripes constantly fail to learn – often with shattering consequences. Freedland describes Remainers in the EU referendum campaign as 'bringing an abacus to a knife fight'. No wonder Remain lost when Leavers were promising we could 'Take back control.' American writer Clay Shirky makes a similar observation about the 2016 American presidential election. Democrats made a 'category error', he says, by patiently noting then-candidate Donald ('Make America Great Again') Trump's contradictions and lies. 'We've brought fact-checkers to a culture war,' he says.

It is the *story of legal aid* (rather than the reality) which has long made it a soft target for cuts and – unless something drastic happens – will likely make it so again during the inevitable post COVID-19 reckoning in public spending.

Whether lawyers like it or not (and however unfair), the story of legal aid told by politicians and much of the media tell goes something like this: it costs too much; it is too easy for the wrong people to get; it's just a racket for lawyers, who use it to make money/mischief;

and, anyway, when there are tough funding decisions to be made, it is not a priority compared with essential services, such as education and health.

It is the story of legal aid which means Boris Johnson was able to respond to the Court of Appeal's legally unremarkable ruling that Shamima Begum must be allowed to return to the UK to challenge the removal of her British citizenship with threats to change legal aid eligibility criteria. He described it as 'odd and perverse' that 'somebody can be entitled to legal aid when they are not only outside the country but have had their citizenship deprived for reasons of national security.'

It is why (according to the *Daily Mail*) 'Almost three quarters of Britons want to stop fugitives like speedboat killer Jack Shepherd getting access to legal aid.' And why, in its report about three siblings jailed for helping one of the failed London tube bombers being 'given' £4.5m in legal aid, the same newspaper includes the entirely irrelevant fact that families of some victims of the Manchester Arena bombing have been paid only £5,500 each by the official compensation scheme.

The story of legal aid is as insidious as it is powerful. It permeates almost every level of the justice system, and taints the working lives of practitioners, day in, day out. It is why unqualified Legal Aid Agency (LAA) caseworkers see fit to second guess the views of lawyers like Community Law Partnership's Mike McIlvaney, nationally recognised for his expertise and experience in housing law, and persistently refuse funding in *Samuels v Birmingham City Council*.

Lawyers were excluded from the pay rises, given to judges, police, prison officers, senior civil servants and others on the justice front-line for their work during COVID-19.

Even after the case won in the Supreme Court (increasing the rights of thousands of tenants across the country), the agency has made no apology and given no explanation for its behaviour. No one's head has rolled; no assurances have been given that caseworker training will be urgently reviewed. It's also why, instead of resigning en masse over the hot mess that is its client and cost management system (CCMS), its 'digital capability team' were nominated by LAA for a civil service skills award.

This publication is filled with examples of how the story of legal aid is playing out at a time when the social justice sector is in peril as never before, and the clients they serve in the direst of straits. Lawyers were designated 'key workers' by government, but not afforded the political recognition and respect afforded health workers and super-market staff. Lawyers were excluded from the pay rises, given to judges, police, prison officers, senior civil servants and others on the justice frontline for their work during COVID-19.

It's why it was it was left to a single criminal defence practitioner Richard Atkinson (rather than the Ministry of Justice or Home Office) to force through introduction of a nationwide protocol for lawyers attending clients in the police station. It's why, as Giles Peaker reports, days after lockdown there were no precautions in place to protect clients, lawyers or court staff attending housing possession hearings. It's why there are no waiting list targets for justice, with one barrister reporting a half-hour magistrates' court hearing scheduled for March 2020 has just been bumped to June 2023. Imagine the furore if people were having to wait that long for essential health services?

It's why every concession made by the LAA to keep the social justice sector afloat through these unprecedented times has been hard won, and the minimum it could do.

The stakes have never been higher for the social justice sector. Survival is not compulsory. The Ministry of Justice is reviewing legal aid sustainability, and no doubt practitioners and those who speak for them are garnering facts and figures to present about the barrage of cuts. Hard statistics undoubtedly have a part to play – but I am 100% sure that on their own they won't be enough to bring about the sea change in political and public thinking needed. We need to start talking less about how little legal aid costs, and more about how much it can do.

Fiona Bawdon is a journalist and campaigner. She is founder of the Legal Aid Lawyer of the Year awards; head of communications at The Legal Education Foundation; and director of Impact - Law for Social Justice.

Baroness Hale of Richmond | The pandemic and the Constitution

In September last year, the UK Supreme Court held that the prorogation of Parliament was not valid, because of its drastic effect upon the ability of Parliament to perform its constitutional function of holding the Government to account at a crucial time in the nation's history. Parliament has three constitutional functions – to pass laws, to vote the Government the money it needs to run the country, and to hold the Government to account for how it does that. In March this year, almost exactly six months later, Parliament surrendered these functions in the face of the COVID-19 pandemic.

It passed the Contingencies Fund Act 2020, which gave the Treasury a massive £260 billion to spend as it decreed. It passed the Coronavirus Act 2020, which gave the Government sweeping powers to change existing laws in response to the emergency and to manage the effects of the pandemic. That Act allowed the Chancellor to introduce the hugely expensive furlough scheme without Parliamentary scrutiny of its details and how it interacted with other employment legislation.

But most of the lockdown has been done, not under that Act, but under the Public Health (Control of Disease) Act 1984. The Health Protection (Coronavirus Restrictions) (England) Regulations 2020 were made under that Act while Parliament was in recess and unable to scrutinize them. These Regulations closed down hotels, restaurants, pubs, cinemas and theatres, hair salons and barbers, places of worship, and much more. They also imposed severe restrictions on our freedom of movement: 'no person may leave the place where they are living without reasonable excuse' – some examples of what would be a reasonable excuse were given, such as shopping, taking exercise and seeking medical help, but there could be others. And they prohibited 'gatherings' of more than two people in a public place.

But a great deal of what the public was told they could or could not do was not in the Regulations. It was just in Government guidance. Some of this suggested what the Regulations meant – for example, taking 'one form of exercise a day' when in fact the Regulation had no such limit. Some of it was instructing people on 'social distancing' which is not in the Regulations at all.

The Regulations did contain draconian powers for the police and some others to enforce the lockdown, for example, by ordering people to go home and taking them there by force if need be. They created new criminal offences of disobeying the Regulations or police orders; they gave wide new powers of arrest to the police, as well as the power to issue fixed penalty notices to people they thought had disobeyed the law.

It is not surprising that the police were as confused as the public as to what was law and what was not. How many of us knew what the relevant Regulations were, let alone what they said?

It is not surprising that the police were as confused as the public as to what was law and what was not. How many of us knew what the relevant Regulations were, let alone what they said? Who were we to quarrel if the police said that we could or could not do things? A certain Government adviser obviously did know what the Regulations were and what they said. Others might also have felt that they had a 'reasonable excuse' for doing something like he did. But they did not do it, either because they did not know the law and just abided by what they were told, or because they thought it was not safe. Hence the outcry that there was one law for those in power and another law for the rest of us. There isn't. But that's how it felt to many. The problem is that laws often have to be nuanced with concepts like 'reasonable excuse' whereas Government messaging in times of crisis has to be crystal clear.

Parliament has now resumed much of its role in holding the Government to account – but it did surrender control to the Government at a crucial time. Maybe this was inevitable. Maybe the lockdown and its severe consequences – so much worse for some people than for others – were inevitable or at least the best solution that could be devised in the circumstances. My plea is that we get back to a properly functioning Constitution as soon as we possibly can.

Baroness Hale of Richmond is a former President and Justice of the Supreme Court of the United Kingdom.

Frederick Wilmot-Smith | 'If we want things to stay as they are, things will have to change'

The most famous line in Giuseppe Tomasi di Lampedusa's *The Leopard* is spoken not by the titular Prince of Salina but his nephew, Tancredi Falconeri. Both Prince and nephew face an urgent practical question: how should they, noblemen, respond to Garibaldi's forces which are sweeping Sicily? Tancredi, younger and more adaptable, tells the Prince, 'If we want things to stay as they are, things will have to change.'

Lawyers are conservative in nature. This is not mere vested interest but a necessary character trait: we spend our days trying to recover the (imagined or real) value of the past. We invoke past political acts – for example, the pronouncements of legislators, judges or contracting parties – as justifications for present decisions. Facing the prospect of law after COVID-19, then, it is tempting for the lawyer, like Tancredi, to consider what must change to ensure continuity.

This is a dangerous temptation. While the Prince and Tancredi both wished to retain things of value, things which could be lost under the harsh industrial and market forces of modernity, that wish was entwined with their defence of their status and privilege. When the past is feudal, conservation is necessarily inegalitarian. So, it is opportune to ask, particularly at a time like this, what we want to change and what we want to stay the same.

My own view is that certain features of the legal system can only be justly conducted face-to-face, in public courts. There are practical reasons, of course. Clients often do not understand what is happening, and it is easier to explain and to comfort – they can be scared as well as confused – when you are able to speak to them in person. But even if all practical objections could be swept away, the kinds of force legal systems enact – people lose their liberty, children are separated from their parents, businesses are bankrupted – cannot be justified to their subjects over a telephone or Zoom call.

Or so I have argued; I can't hope to convince you of that here. If I am right, certain aspects of the justice system can be conducted remotely; certain aspects cannot. There is no shortcut to a detailed consideration of every situation: distrust simplicity. This consideration must, of course, be informed by a proper understanding of the value of the justice system. The more valuable the interests at stake, the less likely it is that the matter can justly be conducted remotely. And I mean *valuable* – not expensive. Certain proceedings in the commercial court might be worth many millions while still being simple to resolve and of scant moral import. By contrast, decisions over personal liberty or parents' rights to see their children – to choose two of many possible examples – should not be conducted remotely.

In making these arguments, we face a grave difficulty: too many have surrendered too much in their thought and talk. The justice system has become a 'service' – as if adjudication over rights was akin to the hospitality industry.

In making these arguments, we face a grave difficulty: too many have surrendered too much in their thought and talk. The justice system has become a 'service' – as if adjudication over rights was akin to the hospitality industry. Claims of justice are now mere 'disputes' to 'resolve', a trend accompanied by pushes for 'mediation', a system of 'dispute resolution' with no regard to the justice of the claims. The nadir is the judiciary's celebration of the justice system's wealth-generating potential. All this betrays a view of law as a market commodity, its objects to be distributed according to the slick right of capital.

Garibaldi's forces overthrew the Kingdom of the Two Sicilies. But Tancredi marries money and maintains his status, as does the Prince. In this, they manage only to maintain injustice – their wealth and status – in the face of a new order which is itself unjust, too. Maybe there's a warning here. Those who preach the market argot are revolutionaries: our system promises equality and justice, not economic efficiency. But there has always been a chasm between the promise and the practice of our system and we should seek, in the years ahead, to maintain that promise and convert it into reality. We must not, in seeking to preserve the legal system's value, entrench its flaws: if we want things to stay as they are, things will have to change.

Fred Wilmot-Smith is a barrister at Brick Court Chambers.

Chris Minnoch | What happens when a system has been starved for years on end

When the nation looks back at this time of tragedy there will be certain aspects that will be forever ingrained in the public consciousness. It is safe to say however that the government's response to the crisis in the justice system is very unlikely to be one of those things. Black cabbies won't regale us with tales of heroic lawyers forced to work at risk in heaving police station cells. Red tops won't publish exposés about those detained against their will in hospitals being denied legal advice. And few will care that there was an extra zero added to the backlogs in the civil and criminal courts. And who will recall that it became increasingly impossible to get advice about mounting debts, or employment rights, or how to challenge yet another crappy Department of Work and Pension or Home Office decision? And that's not because the public doesn't care, but because justice just doesn't register. Not justice in the sense of fundamental principles of fairness and equality and ensuring that rights are not just rhetoric but can be enforced and protected. The Conservative Party manifesto made that clear before the last election. They equated justice with prisons, police and punishment. And they won.

But the PPE debacles, abandonment of care homes and the devastating and disproportionate impact on BAME communities are no surprise at all to legal aid lawyers. They deal with the consequences of poverty, discrimination and inequality on a daily basis. They rise each day and steel themselves for that next emergency judicial review to help someone recover their basic rights or entitlements. They fight against systems that have unfairness and illegality designed into them. And they feed their experiences on behalf of the voiceless into organisations like ours so that we can amplify those voices as we attempt to convince ministers and civil servants that justice really does matter. That the justice system is in crisis: its physical infrastructure crumbling; its principles corrupted by neglect; its position as a cornerstone of a fair and democratic society eroded by decades of deliberate government malnourishment.

That the justice system is in crisis: its physical infrastructure crumbling; its principles corrupted by neglect; its position as a cornerstone of a fair and democratic society eroded by decades of deliberate government malnourishment.

And then a pandemic hits (cue a cartoon 'Kapow!') and we begin to see what happens when a system has been starved for years on end. The lawyers and caseworkers who prop up the system have asked the government for help because the fragility of the sector has been exposed for all to see, if only they would look. Trusts and foundations looked, and they rallied round to save ailing charities, and the government followed suit. But what of the much larger group of social justice lawyers in private practice? Will they still be here to fight for the marginalised and disenfranchised when the inevitable post-lockdown tidal wave of legal problems comes crashing home? As they have been for victims of domestic abuse, those detained and those accused throughout the crisis? When the courts re-open and the inquests and inquiries commence? So far, the government's response to a legal aid sector in desperate need of financial support seems to have been based on the joke 'what do you throw to a drowning lawyer. . . .?' But we are starting to see chinks of light as the government has opened up conversations about 'sustainability' and 'recovery'. Will we see the action and investment needed to back-up those conversations? Watch this space.

Chris Minnoch is CEO of the Legal Aid Practitioners Group (LAPG).

Nic Madge | We would make a difference

My generation, the Baby Boomers, have failed. We have failed appallingly, disastrously. We were born at the best possible time and had everything; good secondary education open to all; free university education (generous maintenance grants; no fees); a National Health Service which cared for us and was eliminating premature death; almost full employment; no wars and no national military service; exciting foreign travel; sexual liberation; a significant improvement in career opportunities for women; revolutions in technology, especially IT. We were free to do almost anything we wanted. There was still much wrong with society – inequality, racism, discrimination, poverty – but we were enthusiastically marching through the sunny uplands. Onwards and upwards. Bob Dylan sang 'the times they are a-changin' and we believed him. We would make a difference. We already lived in a 'welfare state' (think about the meaning of those words), but we would make society a better place.

Our failure became obvious to anyone who cared to look, but the COVID-19 pandemic has brutally ripped off the coverings which concealed some of the problems. The disaster which is the infrastructure of this country is now open for all to see. We have the worst government of my life-time – incompetent, amoral, dishonest – during a crisis which requires the best of governments. But the malaise goes far deeper than the politicians. The public sector has been decimated; savage cuts, year on year; transfer of many functions to the private sector; poor management; low pay and low morale. Despite the dedication and sacrifice (sometimes, tragically, with their lives) of its workers and carers, the pandemic has demonstrated the inability of the NHS to prevent avoidable death; its lack of planning; the running down of resources; inadequate supply chains; a lack of basic equipment such as PPE; and poor decision-making (failure to prepare in January and February; delay in implementing the lockdown in March; and transferring hospital patients to care homes without testing them). The state is responsible for the unnecessary deaths of thousands of people. It is not simply a failure of politicians. It is a combined failure of politicians, civil servants, advisers and the structure which should be supporting them and implementing decisions.

The justice sector does not generally kill people, but it can and does wreck lives. There are clear parallels with the NHS. The courts and tribunals, legal advice and representation have suffered in just the same way. Their 'austerity' cuts have been among the most savage in government. One incident illustrates the woeful malfunctioning of the courts. I was sitting as a judge in a major London court. There was a roof leak. Nothing was done. The court had dispensed with the maintenance man who fixed the boilers and carried out minor repairs. The large outside company which was contracted to maintain the building ignored the leak. Predictably, after several months of inaction, the ceiling of the kitchen underneath the leak collapsed. The kitchen was unusable. Catering services for jurors, the public and advocates were suspended. More months passed before the Ministry of Justice and HM Courts & Tribunals Service (HMCTS) called a meeting, which I attended. The civil servant chairing the meeting announced that its purpose was to 'establish clarity and understanding'. NO! The purpose was to fix the bloody roof leak! I lost patience. When, two days later, nothing had been done, I went onto the roof with a security guard and an old Tesco carrier bag and removed the dead leaves which had been blocking a down-pipe from a valley gutter. In five minutes, using a modicum of common sense and initiative, I had cured a roof leak which had lasted for months. That was not an isolated incident. It is symptomatic of the mismanagement within HMCTS.

For many, society is broken. It is in pieces. We need to re-build it. Many parts of the court system are literally broken. The legal aid and advice system is failing. There are huge advice deserts. Thousands of vulnerable people lack representation. We, as a society, are not ensuring justice for all. There may be justice for the rich and powerful, but the legal system is no longer protecting the weak.

We, as a society, are not ensuring justice for all. There may be justice for the rich and powerful, but the legal system is no longer protecting the weak.

The cause of the problem is long-standing. It dates back forty years to Thatcher and

Reagan; to Joseph and Friedman. Thatcher said, 'there's no such thing as *society*'. Economically, politically, structurally, she shifted the country far to the right. Despite Labour governments since, until this year, economic policies have remained essentially Thatcherite. The centre ground of Butskellism has never been regained. All governments have been terrified of raising taxes. Comparing Ted Heath and Ed Miliband, whose economic policies put a greater portion of GDP into the welfare state? As my mother used to say, 'you don't get what you don't pay for.' If anything good comes out of the COVID-19 pandemic, it may be that finally we realise that we need big, competent government which can plan, organise and care for our welfare. There are many state functions which cannot be left to a poorly regulated private sector which places profit above everything else.

So, the first step towards building, or re-building, a fair and accessible justice system is a recognition that it will cost money; far, far more money than can be realised by the misguided policy of selling off the most valuable court buildings and cutting staff and judicial sittings. There has to be a political will to raise taxes, not only for reconstruction but also for the day-to-day running of fair and efficient processes. Yes, improved IT and some remote hearings have a role to play. We cannot be seen to be Luddites, but there are serious doubts about what the current Court Modernisation Programme will deliver. Without proper evaluation and fundamental change, there is a real risk that it will exclude many vulnerable people from justice.

Second, we must recognise that it is now too late to reform the existing legal aid scheme and Legal Aid Agency. Twenty years ago, that might have been possible. No longer. We need to start again from scratch. Although, in theory, a system of public finance to enable private firms to provide legal aid work is capable of providing a good, economical service, the current system failed even before 'the reforms' which wrecked it. We have to accept that there was abuse by a minority of providers. Some barristers (who would benefit from the grant of legal aid certificates), when providing initial advice, inflated the prospects of success unrealistically, with the result certificates were granted in weak cases. Sometimes, district judges were insufficiently robust in reducing excessive costs claims in civil cases. And there can be no possible justification for the Criminal Defence Service paying, in 2004/2005 individual barristers the sums of (gross) £755,000, £766,000, £902,000 and £1.2m (*The Independent*, 24 April 2006). Perhaps, the best model would be a new, national, publicly funded legal service, modelled on existing law centres. It should not be a monolithic, centrally run service, but instead each centre should be independent and locally managed. Salaries for solicitors, barristers and paralegals should be competitive and in line with reasonable private practice earnings to ensure that able and committed lawyers are employed.

Third, there must be reform of substantive law. Too much of it is too complex. If, as is the case, many lawyers do not understand the law outside their own specialist areas, what prospect is there of the public understanding it? Legal resources are wasted due to its complexity. Key areas should be codified, using simple, plain English so that citizens can understand their basic rights.

We cannot fiddle while Rome burns. We should not tinker with a broken structure. We need to build a new justice system within a restored welfare state.

Nic Madge is a retired circuit judge.

A District Judge | Disengaged from the process

The impact of COVID-19 has been felt in every aspect of life as we know it, but for many the effect on the justice system has had negligible impact. But there are of course thousands of people who are already engaged in court proceedings or who were about to become embroiled in matters making their way through the courts. The media coverage on the courts in this context has focussed, understandably, on the criminal justice system and, specifically, jury trials.

I can only comment on matters from the civil and family law angle, sitting exclusively in those jurisdictions in the County Court.

Save for exceptional circumstances it was been accepted at the outset that attendances in a court building should not take place, for the safety of the public and the staff.

As an alternative and to keep the justice system moving remote hearings have had to be introduced. When the first lockdown announcements were made, we had to initially pause, regroup and rearrange our working practices to cater for fewer support staff available, logistical issues of commuting to courts for judges, professionals and parties. In the main much has been achieved. But there has been a cost.

There has undoubtedly been a cost to welfare and well-being. It seems to be acknowledged that remote hearings do not always proceed smoothly, that they are more challenging to conduct, control and engage in for all participants. They are tiring both mentally and physically.

There has been confusion as to which platforms can be used and by whom which has added to the stress.

Some cases have been heard over a few days successfully, but there is usually a context to that. The high-end work conducted in the commercial courts and in the High Court etc with the additional resources available have had the most success. By contrast at the low end of the spectrum there have been major difficulties in how litigants whether represented or in person have engaged in their

There has undoubtedly been a cost to welfare and well-being. It seems to be acknowledged that remote hearings do not always proceed smoothly, that they are more challenging to conduct, control and engage in for all participants.

hearings. Many colleagues have been left floored by the conduct and attitude of some when they are 'at the hearing' or left frustrated by constant failures to have parties either get in to remote hearings or stay in for the duration.

A survey carried out by the District Bench and which was shared not only with the senior judiciary, but the Nuffield research commissioned by the President of the Family Division PFD exposed the pressures faced in keeping the system going through this period.

Litigants have reportedly felt disengaged from the process and find it difficult to articulate themselves either on video or on the phone. There are also those that view the remote hearing as something that should fit in with their other activities. I have heard of litigants dealing with their hearings while waiting in supermarket queues, and a colleague had one hearing where the claimant was serving customers in his shop at the same time and was clearly not properly concentrating.

There have been multiple instances of parties in domestic violence or children cases having to discuss those cases in the presence of children or other family members. Even, in some instances two individuals engaged in litigation being in the same house, without the obvious safety measures that a court building offers.

There is also a misguided assumption by HM Courts & Tribunals Service (HMCTS) that everyone has extensive opportunities to connect through technology, not recognising with just a smartphone there are costs of data provision which some cannot afford.

Every successful hearing has been seized upon by HMCTS and some members of the profession as a vindication of the remote way of working and certainly it has given HMCTS a new lease of life in trying again to push on the original agenda of the court reform process which had at its core, a transition to video hearings becoming the default option, with fewer physical courts. The message they champion is that if remote hearings work for some (ignoring the specifics of individual cases) they can work for all.

While we can acknowledge what can be achieved there must be caution as to where this could lead if HMCTS see the celebrated successes as their green light to accelerate and impose a way of working that will offer justice on the cheap.

More challenges will follow as we try and clear the backlog of cases that have been held up in the system, while at the same time addressing the rush of cases which, inevitably, have been held back from issue. It will necessitate an acknowledgement from HMCTS that the pool of part-time judges must be engaged quickly and efficiently, and that budgetary restrictions cannot be allowed to slow down that process.

In going forward, we can perhaps take heart from the fact that our staff have shown a commitment to the cause, despite their anxieties of coming in to work while so many were able to work from home and showing their willingness to quickly adopt new ways of working. We also learned much of the remote process and while we would never advocate hearings conducted in this way as a being the default option, we can introduce options into our daily lists where justified and practical.

I think it is also fair to say that the way we have operated during the pandemic has brought home the importance of the physical interaction on a daily basis, that should never be taken for granted and an appreciation of the roles that the professionals, the court staff and judges play in trying to best serve the public.

The author has been sitting as a deputy, and full-time, district judge for over 20 years having been in practice as a predominantly legal aid solicitor in a traditional high street practice.

Young Legal Aid Lawyers | We must all speak with one voice

COVID-19 and the Black Lives Matter movement have laid bare societal inequalities that harm our clients. But we must also address how sustained legal aid cuts, and senior legal aid lawyers' responses to them, have deepened inequalities within the sector. Urgent action is needed to ensure that going into legal aid is a viable career path; one that is open to anyone with dedication and talent regardless of the colour of their skin or the size of their parents' bank balance.

Young Legal Aid Lawyers (YLAL) exists to campaign for a sustainable legal aid system, to promote social mobility and diversity within the sector and to provide a support network for aspiring and junior legal aid lawyers. Unsurprisingly, we have been working on overdrive since COVID-19 struck.

Before COVID-19, paralegals, trainees and junior legal aid lawyers were overworked and underpaid. Cuts to legal aid have led to the 'paralegalisation' of the profession, with many firms using the carrot of a training contract to keep talented aspiring lawyers working for years as paralegals, often at under the living wage. The situation upon qualification is not much better, with low wages, vicarious trauma from supporting our clients and unrealistic billing targets persisting. It is not sustainable for someone in their 30s to work every hour of the day and yet to be barely earning enough to pay their rent in a shared house. Given this situation, it is not surprising that we are seeing the attrition of talented lawyers from the profession, particularly those from diverse backgrounds.

During lockdown, YLAL undertook two rapid consultations to gather evidence of the impact of COVID-19 on our members. Hundreds of junior legal aid lawyers responded. At the height of lockdown, a quarter of our members were expected to put themselves at risk of infection due to their workplace preventing them from working fully remotely. Almost 80% reported fears about their job security. Furloughed staff rarely had their income topped up to their full salaries. Many had heightened anxieties because communication from law firm partners and senior barristers had been poor. YLAL also surveyed and advocated for its student members. We stand in complete solidarity with disabled Bar students who have not been provided with reasonable adjustments by the Bar Standards Board.

YLAL is active in campaigning against legal aid cuts during the pandemic. When the government introduced new regulations in response to COVID-19 that changed the fixed fee for asylum and immigration legal aid work, we launched one of our biggest campaigns ever. We approached the Shadow Legal Aid Minister and explained that the regulations would prevent those with the most complex cases, such as victims of trafficking and LGBT+ asylum-seekers, from accessing justice. The Opposition tabled a fatal motion to the regulations. Our #APrayerForLegalAid campaign persuaded 130 MPs from six parties to back the motion. That was only part of our campaign. We also worked with Liberty, the Bar Council, ILPA, the Refugee and Migrant Children's Consortium and the anti-trafficking sector to make as much noise as possible about the threat to access to justice. We produced a report, 'A Sector at Breaking Point: Justice Denied for Victims of Trafficking' that was relied upon by anti-trafficking charities and the Independent Anti-Slavery Commissioner to push the government to change its position. The report was also important evidence in litigation challenging the regulations. Our campaign was featured in *Legal Cheek*, *The Independent* and other press and, most importantly, we secured a meeting with the legal aid minister where we explained the impact of the regulations on access to justice. On 11 August 2020, the government conceded judicial review claims and accepted the unlawfulness of the regulations. The litigation and campaigning against the regulations show how much legal aid lawyers can achieve when they take a stand and work together.

Going forward, we must continue to campaign collaboratively for a sustainable legal aid system. Legal aid cuts are an existential threat to the future of the profession and access to justice. We must all speak with one voice and demand more funding: be that reform of legal aid rates or bringing areas back into scope. However, we must also have difficult conversations

We must all speak with one voice and demand more funding: be that reform of legal aid rates or bringing areas back into scope.

with our colleagues. If we want to have a diverse and sustainable pipeline of junior legal aid lawyers, the impact of the cuts should fall on those with the broadest shoulders. Currently, pain that is visited upon the legal aid sector is disproportionately felt by the most junior. That is totally unacceptable and must change.

Young Legal Aid Lawyers (YLAL) is a group of aspiring and junior lawyers committed to practising in those areas of law that have traditionally been publicly funded.

Mary-Rachel McCabe | Well-being for lawyers: feast or famine

On 4 March 2020 I had what is called a 'practice development review meeting' with my clerks. It is, as you might imagine, an annual meeting with my clerks to review my practice: do you like the work you are doing? Have you got enough work? Are you earning enough money? Do you want to branch into any other areas of practice? That sort of thing. The notes from the meeting (prepared by my senior clerk) included the following:

> M-R's practice is very busy at the moment and a little on the side of too busy. M-R would like to be in court no more than three times per week and the clerks will block her diary out accordingly. Work/life balance is important to M-R.

At the time of the meeting, I was exceptionally busy and had been since returning to work after the Christmas break. I was desperate for some reprieve from the relentlessness, so when my clerks duly blocked out my diary for two days a week for the following six months, I breathed a sigh of relief: the work/life balance I had carefully cultivated previously would quickly return.

Fast forward two weeks and every hearing that I had in my diary for the following fortnight had disappeared. The parties had reached agreement or sought adjournments because they didn't want to travel to court unnecessarily. COVID-19 was tightening its grip on our country, and my diary was completely empty.

The 'feast or famine' nature of the publicly funded Bar will be familiar to many. I have lost count of how many times I have been advised by my older and wiser colleagues to enjoy the quiet periods as they will never last long, and once the 5am starts begin again 'you will regret not savouring the breathing space.'

Despite this, as lockdown was announced, courts closed and the empty weeks in my diary stretched ahead, I – like countless others in similar or worse positions – began to worry about my income. Rather than enjoying the downtime I panic-filled those weeks in late March/early April with unpaid work. I read the Coronavirus Act 2020 (all 348 pages of it) from start to finish. I wrote a blog about it. I spoke at a 'webinar' about the impact of the Coronavirus Act on adult social care. I gave pro bono advice to solicitors who were worried about the sweeping changes to the law being introduced. I wrote another blog. I spoke at another webinar.

By mid-April, as my instructing solicitors and the courts began to get to grips with remote working, new cases started to trickle in and my diary began to fill up. My panic was averted, at least for the time being.

Lockdown learnings

I believe that nothing in life is absolute. Nothing is completely either one thing or another – completely bad or completely good. The negative impact of lockdown on lawyers is well-documented: the challenges of juggling caring responsibilities with our high-pressured work, jobs lost, incomes demolished, isolation, the lost opportunity to talk a tricky case through with a colleague at the water filter in the office.

But amidst the awfulness of what we are going through collectively and individually, there are unexpected compensations that – I hope – we will treasure for life.

Last year, I wrote an article for *Counsel* magazine about well-being at the Bar and the challenges of saying no to work overload as a junior legal aid barrister. Reflecting on August at the Bar – when juniors are asked by their clerks to stick around to cover the work of more senior barristers who are on holiday – I wrote:

> *I cannot describe a 'typical' day because there is no such thing. Throughout August, however, my days began at 5am, involved a long train journey to somewhere in England, a packet of mini-cheddars from the court vending machine for lunch, and crawling into bed at 11pm, with the following day's alarm set for 4.45am because I was travelling somewhere even further away.*

This August will look completely, gloriously different. My new routine throughout lockdown has involved waking up at 7.30am; doing some morning yoga in the kitchen; enjoying breakfast and lunch at home; going for regular runs in the afternoon; planning, cooking and eating delicious meals in the evenings; watching films and box sets that I had been planning to watch for years but 'never had the time'; seeing my neighbours doing their daily exercise in the park instead of the gym; walking along the canal and watching the geese and goslings swimming in a row.

I have been momentarily liberated from the frenetic pace of life at the junior Bar and my physical and mental health is all the better for it.

I hope, therefore, that one thing we can all reflect on following this extraordinary period is just how much time we spend on work and how we push aside the things we should be doing for ourselves. Do we really need to work 12-14 hours every day? Must we work every weekend? Do we need to attend events in the evening every week? What will happen if we don't?

I have been momentarily liberated from the frenetic pace of life at the junior Bar and my physical and mental health is all the better for it.

I have always argued that the best way of coping with the challenges of working as a legal aid lawyer is to be able to say 'no' to overwork, so that we have time out for self-preservation. Regardless of the hours we work, we will always have to carry the weight of our clients' trauma, endure the stress of propping up a legal aid and justice system that is on its knees and suffer silently through bullying from our opponents and judges.

But having sufficient sleep, time in the evenings and weekends to ourselves and to spend with the people who are important to us, time in nature and time for reflection will help to cultivate the physical and mental energy needed to keep fighting for justice for our clients.

Lockdown has given this to many of us. So, when the time comes to get out of our homes, back to the office and back into court, let's not forget the positive impact this period has had on our wellbeing by jumping straight back onto the path to burnout.

Mary-Rachel McCabe is a barrister at Doughty Street Chambers.

Dr Daniel Newman | Greed will be all that stands in the way of change

In academia, the coronavirus crisis has shone a light on issues around accessibility. It has shown that things can be done differently and in a more socially just, equitable manner.

The academy is an unwelcoming place for those who do not fit into the neat (neo)liberal individualist ideal of someone who will go anywhere and do anything to further their career. There are many barriers that exclude different groups.

This includes people who are disabled or neurodivergent, have chronic illnesses or mental health problems. It also includes people with caring responsibilities – especially but not exclusively women, as well as those from working class backgrounds and people working on precarious contracts.

Academia can work to lock people out. For example, there is an obsession with travelling to conferences, workshops and seminars that is unaffordable to some, impractical for those with other obligations and potentially impossible due to a range of health conditions.

Yet getting known by others in the field is vital for developing reputations, for getting invited to contribute to proposals and for developing a sense of self-worth as a scholar. Such events can also lead to the forming of vital support networks that scholars grow with as they progress through the ranks.

Traditionally, though, opportunities to present and participate remotely are few and far between. This can hold people back.

With coronavirus, the shift to remote working has been swift – and effective enough to keep academia going. It was stressful for many, with a steep learning curve, but it was done.

Everything moved online. Most pressing for the everyday business of the university, this involved teaching and administration-related activity; classes, supervisions, open days, meetings and committees.

But suddenly research-related activity was online also. The big conferences are planning their virtual meetings, the workshops are conducted using computer software, invited seminar talks from across the globe are delivered from the speaker's bedroom.

Now, the lecturer with young children and no childcare support can present their paper to the experts in their field. And, the autistic postgraduate who could not make the commute to participate in a meeting with their peers has access to comradeship and feedback.

Many scholars are facing up to what it is like to have to work from home, shut off from their usual networks; an enforced empathy with those for whom academia was already a struggle. They are working out what it means to have to communicate remotely and how to negotiate relationships at a distance.

Academic institutions, from individual schools and universities to funding organisations and membership associations, for years have been giving demands to improve accessibility short shrift. Meetings are booked in buildings that are totally unsuitable for wheelchairs because grand enough to produce the desired image or the fees required from those attending in person mean that online participation is dismissed as impossible, pricing out those who cannot afford it.

The move online – and the speedy acceptance of these new ways of working – has created opportunities. The social justice implications are massive for those who have traditionally come up against a ceiling on their academic ambitions.

Online working is not perfect. It can be socially isolating for those not used to home-working and not all will have sufficient technology to participate, working from different time-zones can be problematic, accessibility practices still need to be improved for many health conditions or caring responsibilities, and it should not be assumed that video calls are easy for everyone. But it does offer improvement – and those who have felt shut down and ignored for so long are justified if they feel resentful that suddenly work-arounds are found. It is palpably wrong that it would take a pandemic that disrupts everyone to enact the kind of reforms that some have spent years shouting for.

And it is optimistic to suppose that practices will not just pivot back to business-as-usual – or as close as possible – because the financial imperatives of contemporary academia have become so all-consuming. But there has been increasing resistance to the neoliberal university, as seen in the strength of recent industrial actions that this is a moment to build on.

We have seen it is possible to do things differently and any academics who care about social justice should work to ensure that academia after the crisis is more open and welcoming of those who could not make the old system work for them.

There is no reasonable excuse for not carrying forward the advancements in accessibility that have been made during the coronavirus crisis. Yes, many people will want to host a meeting to see their old friends or jet away to an exotic location for a talk, but such demands cannot justifiably be held up as the norm we expect of academics anymore.

Greed will be all that stands in the way of change, a continuation of the privileging of profit above people that has hurt so many scholars, stalling careers and making some think that they cannot enter the academy. We have seen it is possible to do things differently and any academics who care about social justice should work to ensure that academia after the crisis is more open and welcoming of those who could not make the old system work for them.

Those of us who write about social justice causes will not show the courage of our convictions unless we promote socially just practices like this in our field. And the opportunity to expand academia to include the insights of those who have been for too long marginalised is a crucial one to ensure that scholarship reflects and understands the challenges people face today.

Dr Daniel Newman is senior lecturer in law at Cardiff University.

Dr Jacqueline Kinghan and Rachel Knowles | There has never been a more important time to listen

University law schools play an important role in teaching students about law in society and the impact of unresolved legal problems on those experiencing discrimination and disadvantage. Law school clinics have grown exponentially in recent years but have always faced a number of challenges: they require investment; have been traditionally less welcome in research intensive environments; and can be perceived to bring risk to large and complex institutions. There are comparatively few academics in areas of social welfare law meaning fewer graduate students coming through the system and lower inclination in wider law school culture to support the study of social welfare subjects. The changes brought about by the Solicitors Qualifying Exam (SQE) also mean there will no longer be examination in any areas of social welfare law. Yet, university clinics are a valuable piece in the puzzle of meeting access to justice needs post-LASPO. Research also tells us that clinical opportunities are particularly important for those students who come to law school with social justice orientated goals. We know it can help them to feel less isolated in environments that are often geared towards corporate law; and can foster critical engagement with the both the theory and practice of access to justice to take into their future careers.

How then has COVID-19 impacted upon university clinical legal advice provision? Like many other law centres and law firms, moving to remote working at short notice for lockdown in March 2020 posed problems that required swift resolution. Clinics grappled with students accessing case management systems remotely while maintaining standards of confidentiality and GDPR compliance; as well as quickly becoming accustomed to remote hearings and the heightened needs of clients in often unnerving and unsettling online environments. Lucy Yeatman, co-chair of the Clinical Legal Education Organisation (CLEO) says that all clinics have been on a 'steep learning curve' since lockdown. Many placement and partnership activities in host organisations have simply been unable to continue as planned and Lucy comments that 'student support services such as helpdesks and McKenzie friend services in courts have ground to a halt.' She says that even when the courts reopen, the universities will have their own risk assessment procedures to follow which might hinder re-establishing advice provision. As she laments, 'there is still so much uncertainty it is likely that services for clients will be affected.'

The uncertainty from the university perspective largely relates to anticipated student numbers and how programmes will be delivered. As law schools consider whether teaching should be exclusively online, it is unclear the extent to which students will be able to support the delivery of clinical advice and in what capacity. For most law school clinics an entire re-think of supervision models is therefore underway. From a supervisor's perspective, it is of course much easier to gently intervene and guide a student who might be going off task or getting things wrong when you are in the same room observing their work. Effective clinical environments also allow students to feel comfortable asking questions, to air their concerns and communicate when they think they might have made a mistake. Likewise, students tend to build their own learning communities; they learn from one another and support each other. There is no easy way to recreate this remotely.

The pandemic presents an opportunity for universities to be more flexible and responsive to support the experiential learning of their students during this crisis.

Many law school clinics across the UK are working hard to overcome these challenges and are thinking carefully and creatively about solutions. Clinical staff need allocated time and resource to adapt their training and supervision; and to respond to ever changing access to justice needs as a result of the pandemic. The pandemic presents an opportunity for universities to be more flexible and responsive to support the experiential learning of their students during this crisis. It is hoped that beyond the pandemic, they will realise the importance of embedding social welfare law as a field of study in order to play their part in sustaining access to justice.

After almost a decade in clinical legal education we know that law students have the capacity to be highly engaged in some of the most urgent and important social justice issues of our times. There has never been a more important time to listen; to harness their passion; and to create opportunities that will help foster the next generation of social justice lawyers.

Dr Jacqueline Kinghan is senior lecturer in law and social justice at Newcastle Law School. Rachel Knowles is senior teaching fellow at UCL Faculty of Laws.

Jamie Burton | Let's lay the foundations we need to build the better society we want tomorrow

The COVID-19 pandemic is not even the first global crisis to befall us this century. Surging from west to east this time, the Global Financial Crisis was as terrifyingly portentousness in 2007/8 as the pandemic is now. True of both of these pervasive crises is that their ultimate toll will be as much a result of how we react to the threat as the threat itself.

Perhaps this is where the similarities will end, however. For the moment at least, Boris Johnson professes it would be a 'mistake' to repeat the austerity imposed the last time we faced a crisis-inflated deficit It is easy to understand why: many prominent experts, including the International Monetary Fund, believe the decade long belt-tightening actually damaged the economy, and by 2014 the then Prime Minister preferred to defend austerity with a moral case rather than any imperative to 'make the numbers add up', while four years later his successor claimed to end it altogether; cuts in public expenditure are probably not compatible with the 'levelling up' promised to many first time Conservative voters in 2019 and, in any event, public attitudes seem to have changed, with recent polling showing growing support for tax rises to pay for a 'kinder, fairer society.' Is the pandemic bringing us together in the way the Financial Crisis divided us?

Rhetorically at least, the pendulum has swung so far back it has skipped a few crises, with today's politicians seeking inspiration from the post-Great Depression/WWII transatlantic collectivism that gave us Roosevelt's New Deal and the Welfare State. Certainly, this moment requires no less ambition. The pandemic has exacerbated acute injustices caused by deep and persistent inequalities across all aspects of economic, social and cultural life. The same groups of people have been hit hardest, again. Without significant intervention these inequities are set to worsen, perhaps irreversibly, as the economic fall-out from the virus increases.

Yet today's legacy makers are overlooking the aspect of the post-WWII international consensus most capable of matching current demands for fundamental change. Built on the inherent dignity of everyone, the Universal Declaration of Human Rights envisioned universal freedom from tyranny *and* want. To incorporate into domestic law all the rights contained in the Declaration (or the specific Covenants ratified since), including the rights to adequate housing, food and basic goods, social security, education, healthcare and just conditions of work, would provide an essential foundation from which a fairer and more just society could be built and sustained.

The pandemic has exacerbated acute injustices caused by deep and persistent inequalities across all aspects of economic, social and cultural life.

Enforceable economic, social and cultural rights would constitute a genuine transfer of power, resistant to political whim and yet sensitive to economic and social realities. Basic needs would have to be met and resources justly distributed, but with the political choices of the legislature always respected save where undone by objective evidence. Critically, even in times of economic adversity, measures which disproportionately affect the least well off would be prohibited.

Enforceable rights are about much more than litigation, although that is important. When formulated in accordance with the norms of the human rights framework, including the obligation to prioritise the expert views of those directly affected by injustice, policy tends to be evidence based and more effective as a result. Laws designed to solve problems rather than win votes benefit everyone. Populism and human rights are seldom natural allies.

That said, public opinion was on the side of economic and social rights even before COVID-19 took hold and is likely to have grown considerably since. Amidst the hardship, the pandemic has fostered levels of social solidarity not seen in most of our lifetimes. It has reminded us that our society is only ever as strong as its weakest members and that when we act together rather than just for ourselves, we are all better off. But these sentiments are not self-realising. They must be given effect through constitutional change.

In that regard the UK is increasingly out of step with many other modern democracies. Numerous countries have recognised that the indivisibility of human rights means it is not possible to have effective civil and political rights without protecting economic, social and cultural rights too. You simply cannot have one without the other. With moves afoot in Scotland and Wales too, England's citizens are in danger of being left behind.

Long before it was discarded politically, the inadequacies of the austerity program were apparent to the bodies charged with monitoring the UK's compliance with economic and social rights. Despite receiving masses of evidence from the government, three independent UN Committees separately voiced serious concerns about the unjustified adverse impact of many austerity measures on already disadvantaged groups, including woman, children, disabled and Black, Asian and Minority Ethnic people. It is not implausible to suggest that the program would have been different had economic and social rights been part of our law. Would we be living in a society better able to resist the virus as a result?

This is not the last crisis we shall confront. The reforms we make now will determine how robust we are in the face of the next. It was considered vital to promulgate comprehensive human rights protections when we emerged from a global crisis nearly a century ago. Finishing the work of our predecessors now would lay the foundations we need to build the better society we want tomorrow.

Jamie Burton is a barrister at Doughty Street Chambers.

Matthew Evans | EU citizens in the UK

An optimistic reading of immigration in the time of COVID-19 is that the pandemic has created a shift in the public mood and debate on migration in the UK. Those previously (mis) labelled as 'low skilled' workers, such as cleaners and delivery drivers, are now seen as key workers holding the UK together during this period of crisis.

A more pessimistic view is that any shift, if indeed it is real, has not translated into a perceptible change in government policy making, such as re-looking at the latest obsession with 'skills' requirements in the new immigration rules, something significant number of migrant workers in essential occupations simply cannot hope to meet. However, what is clear, is that the pandemic risks creating new problems and uncertainty for those with the most insecure immigration status, including EU citizens who will wonder whether and how they can secure the set of rights which come with EU citizenship.

This short article will concentrate on two very specific issues concerning EU citizens during the current crisis. The first is their ability to access the UK's social assistance scheme during a time of economic crisis and uncertainty. The second is the barriers which they face in returning to their country of residence.

The UK and EU have reached a deal ('the Withdrawal Agreement') setting out the terms of the UK's departure from the EU, which included preserving the rights of EU citizens living in the UK and vice-versa, promising to treat them equally to Brits.

As part of this deal, all EU, EEA and Swiss citizens and their non-EU family members need to apply to the EU Settlement Scheme (EUSS) for a new immigration status before the deadline of 30 June 2021 in order to continue to be able to continue to live lawfully in the UK. The COVID-19 crisis has had a very practical effect on EU citizens trying to apply under the scheme, including the temporary closure of the Home Office Resolution Centre which deals with more complex applications. The difficulties are evidenced by the dramatic fall in applications during the March and April period.

However, COVID-19 has also led to an increasing number of EU citizens living in Britain now having to apply for British benefits for the first time, as many find themselves out of work or with a drastically reduced income. An impact assessment commissioned by Migration Exchange in May 2020 concluded that many EU citizens living in the UK who have lost their income source due to COVID-19 have minimal access to a social safety net.

What has the EUSS got to do with any of this? The answer lies in the fact that EU citizens face significant problems in accessing benefits, because of difficulties evidencing that they pass the 'habitual residence test', which for EU citizens acts as a gateway or more correctly a 'blockade' to accessing social assistance support in the UK. The EUSS has magnified these difficulties for those granted temporary leave to remain/pre-settled status (those EU nationals and family members who have lived in Britain less than five years), as compared to these with indefinite leave/settled status (evidence of residence of more than 5 years).

Before July 2019, those with pre-settled status were also able to satisfy the habitual residence requirement, but the UK government introduced regulations to stop that. Those granted pre-settled status (around 1.4million people or 41% of concluded applications) are now discovering that they are no longer automatically entitled to Universal Credit or other means-tested benefits including housing support. In contrast, someone with 'settled status', automatically satisfies the 'right to reside' requirement of the Habitual Residence test.

EU citizens with pre-settled status must therefore prove their right to reside in an alternative way, such as showing they are a worker or self-employed, tests which the Department of Work and Pensions (DWP) frequently gets wrong. The AIRE Centre has advised a number of EU nationals, who meet the income requirements to apply for benefits, but whose applications are being wrongly rejected. One such case involved Philip (a pseudonym), a Polish citizen with pre-settled status living in the UK. He is a freelance piano tutor and worked in the hospitality industry. He was laid off from his hospitality job in February 2020. He continued as a piano tutor after the pandemic hit the UK. However, his application to Universal Credit was rejected for failing the Habitual Residence test, despite working over 10 hours per week as a tutor. He faced not being able to pay the rent, and it was only after AIRE intervened that the DWP changed their decision and confirmed he was entitled to Universal Credit.

The second issue is that pre-settled status expires after five years. People granted pre-settled status must therefore apply for settled status before then or risk being without legal permission to be in the UK. What many people seem unaware of is the absence of rules relating to time spent outside of the UK. This affects not just people stranded due to border closures across Europe during COVID-19 but also the many EU nationals studying in the UK, who have returned to their home countries, and who are being told by their academic institutions that teaching will be online for the foreseeable future. If they remain outside the UK for more than six months in any 12-month period during the five years it takes to qualify for full settled status, they will generally have to start the five years all over again. The 6-month rule can be extended to 12 months for 'compelling reasons', but at the moment there is no new general exception making allowances for the pandemic. So pre-settled status holders who return to the UK later than the end of this year will be in trouble if they have been gone for more than six months.

As of July 2020, the 1.3 million EU citizens and family members granted pre-settled status have been forced to choose between following government guidance, staying home and falling into destitution, or returning to work and risking their own and public health.

The other important point is that although pre-settled status only lapses through two years of absence from the UK, there are two important caveats to this rule. The first is that a person who has broken their continuous residence period will still need to reapply for pre-settled status when they return to ensure that they can ultimately upgrade to settled status. That is because pre-settled status cannot be renewed or extended, so an interruption will leave the person short of the five years they need to qualify with no way of making up the time. The second caveat is that if the individual returns after 31 December 2020, they may lose the right to upgrade to settled status entirely. This is because of how a 'continuous qualifying period' is defined in Appendix EU. It has to begin before 11pm on that date. If someone with pre-settled status exceeds the permitted absences and returns to the UK after 31 December 2020, they will be unable to restart the settled status clock at all.

As of July 2020, the 1.3 million EU citizens and family members granted pre-settled status have been forced to choose between following government guidance, staying home and falling into destitution, or returning to work and risking their own and public health. The most obvious solution would be to honour the initial commitment which the UK made to EU citizens and to accept pre-settled status and automatic 'right to reside' so that EU citizens and non-EU family members can access social security benefits and homelessness assistance during the pandemic and beyond.

The second, would be to confirm that any breaks in 'continuous residency' caused by COVID-19 do not affect EU citizens' and family members' ability to secure status through the EUSS (or to obtain British citizenship).

Finally, and in the case of any second wave 'lockdown' to ensure that the EUSS application process complies with the Withdrawal Agreement and equality laws so that vulnerable EU citizens and family members are not put at unnecessary risk of infection from COVID-19.

Matthew Evans is director of the AIRE Centre.

Sadat Sayeed | The immigration debate

In these strangest of times, it often feels difficult to conceptualise the world that may exist on 'the other side' of the pandemic. However, there is no doubt that in many areas of politics, law, society and culture, new contested spaces are going to open up in which progressive ideas will have the opportunity to make serious pitches for mainstream political and social acceptance. How we view migrants and immigration control is a perfect example.

For nearly 60 years, since the passing of the Commonwealth Immigrants Act 1962, the general direction of travel in respect of immigration has been largely unidirectional: ever more restrictive controls on immigration and increasingly coercive state machinery deployed to enforce those controls. While it is true to say there have been some countertrends, most notably free movement of people within the EU, the political and media discourse on immigration control has in the main become ever more hostile towards migrants and migration into the UK.

This reached fever pitch in the run up to the EU referendum in 2016, with the centrepiece of the 'Leave' campaign focussed on 'taking back control' of our borders. That narrative was underpinned by strong currents of racism, sometimes overt, extending well beyond the scope of EU migration. Arguably the groundwork for that campaign was laid in the 'hostile environment' policies instituted by Theresa May during her tenure as Home Secretary, aided and abetted by media outlets such as the *Daily Mail,* and which reached a dreadful crescendo with the 2018 Windrush scandal. To a greater or lesser extent, the general election result of December 2019 appeared to represent public endorsement of these policies and narratives, and looked set to usher in a new, even more hostile era of anti-migration politics.

And then came the COVID-19 pandemic. While the focus of the public and the political class has, since the spring, understandably been about fighting the virus and all its horrors, emerging from the crisis are the green shoots of a new conversation about migration and migrants, framed by the principles of compassion and rationality, rather than vitriol and hysteria. This is part of a broader narrative

While the focus of the public and the political class has, since the spring, understandably been about fighting the virus and all its horrors, emerging from the crisis are the green shoots of a new conversation about migration and migrants, framed by the principles of compassion and rationality, rather than vitriol and hysteria.

which has emerged around the value that we as a society place on workers, many of whom are migrants (from both within and beyond the EU), whose work was previously characterised as 'unskilled' but is now universally recognised as 'essential'. In an ICM poll conducted for British Future and the Policy Institute at Kings College London in May 2020, two-thirds of the public (64%) agreed that

The coronavirus crisis has made me value the role of 'low-skilled' workers, in essential services such as care homes, transport and shops, more than before.

There has already been one very significant political victory arising out of this newly framed debate, namely the government's U-turn on the requirement for NHS staff and care workers to pay the controversial NHS surcharge. However, there is no time or space for complacency: on 18 May 2020, the Immigration and Social Security Co-ordination (EU Withdrawal) Bill 2020 passed its second reading. This legislation intends to bring a halt to future EU free movement and in its place introduce a new points-based system for all foreign workers. Home Secretary Priti Patel told MPs that the immigration bill will be 'firmer, fairer and simpler' and 'lay the foundation for a high-wage, high-skill, high-productivity economy.' The most controversial of the proposals is the imposition of a £25,600 minimum salary threshold for aspiring migrants, thereby immediately slicing out of the UK's future inbound migration, the majority of NHS, care sector and other essential workers, who have been so enthusiastically clapped by the public and Tory politicians alike at 8pm every Thursday evening.

While the current government, with a political lineage and future agenda shaped by the narrative of the successful 'Leave' campaign, still has the best part of five years left in power with a very significant majority in Parliament, the unprecedented economic and social upheaval caused by the pandemic means that it is facing increasingly strong and unexpected political crosswinds. One of the topics which seems now up for renewed national debate is the way we, as a society, treat migrants and view immigration.

Against that backdrop, there has never been a more opportune moment to halt and reverse the hitherto inexorable march to the right of the Overton window on migrants and migration. Those who have campaigned for a more just, humane and economically literate immigration system now have everything to play for.

Sadat Sayeed is a barrister at Garden Court Chambers.

Victoria Marks | Human connection

Joanne

Joanne sits in a small room. Alone. There's no comfort from familiar voices on the radio or the distraction of a mindless TV show, as she can't afford either. Another long, empty day stretches ahead. Her phone credit has run out and so has her money. For days now she has spent the hours staring at the wall. She has survived worse; she has survived slavery. But the National Referral Mechanism (NRM) system, which is meant to help her recover, so that she can leave behind a life of abuse and exploitation, has left her trapped: in poverty, without dignity or occupation, dependent once again, this time on the state. It is the middle of 'lockdown' and the NRM have just stopped her money, without warning. Now she has £35.39 to survive on and with no right to work she can't see a way out. With legal representation her subsistence will eventually be reinstated but for several weeks Joanne's life is made immeasurably worse by this; the interminable silence uninterrupted, save for the occasional call from her legal aid solicitor and NRM support worker.

Silvana

As a result of traumatic experiences Silvana lives with intrusive thoughts and hears voices. As the pandemic broke, the Home Office agreed to reconsider her negative trafficking decision. Unfortunately, she was refused a place in an NRM safe-house where there are staff to support survivors of trafficking. This meant that going into 'lockdown' she found herself quite alone, living in a hostel with no regular staff to check on her or coax her out of her room. She was too afraid to go out, not even for essentials. The isolation made Silvana's anxiety worse. She sat up, night after night, vigilant and alert to danger, unable to stop thinking. By day she slumbered, exhausted. Her psychiatric nurse and legal aid solicitor would call her but without human contact she could not engage. Eventually the pressure of her fears was too great, and Silvana was hospitalised.

For many survivors of trafficking, like Joanne and Silvana, legal aid lawyers were a lifeline for their clients during the pandemic, calling to check on their well-being, breaking otherwise uninterrupted isolation. But alongside their legal work, they were, more than ever before, faced with overwhelming human need. Much of this was practical, such as sourcing food and phone credit or accessing welfare benefits, but more often it was emotional: seeking support for clients considering suicide, providing reassurance to those who kept calling when the anxiety became too much or, just listening whilst they cried wordlessly down the phone.

For many survivors of trafficking, like Joanne and Silvana, legal aid lawyers were a lifeline for their clients during the pandemic, calling to check on their well-being, breaking otherwise uninterrupted isolation.

Seeking justice for many survivors has not been possible during the pandemic. Without regular face to face human contact and support those with fragile mental health cannot safely revisit and share traumatic memories of abuse. So often their case will rest on these details, and be supported by a medico-legal report, for which a remote psychological assessment is impossible and inadequate. But this reminds us of what is valuable, what is important, how we achieve justice. At its core our work is about assisting survivors to tell their story. This is often a slow, difficult and traumatic process, which can't be rushed. It involves trust, on both sides, and for most survivors it involves making a human connection. For lawyers, this process can also be difficult; these stories are hard to hear, and you carry them with you.

In a time when so many services have moved online and remote working has become the norm, when courts are embracing technology and remote hearings are all the rage, we must remember that without that human connection and without access to face to face advice, justice for some remains all too remote.

Victoria Marks is a solicitor and director of the Anti-Trafficking and Labour Exploitation Unit (ATLEU).

Brigitta Balogh | Roma people in Europe

While everyone in the world is facing COVID-19, Roma people in Europe continue facing racism on the top of the coronavirus.

Despite several articles and reports that have been published in the past few months about the hardships that Roma people experience, it is safe to say that Roma people are disproportionately affected by COVID-19 across Europe.

On 7 April 2020, the European Union Agency for Fundamental Rights (FRA), the Organization for Security and Co-operation in Europe Office for Democratic Institutions and Human Rights, and the Council of Europe issued statements drawing attention to the disproportionate risks that Romani community faces in relation to contracting COVID-19.

Pointing out earlier research, the statement highlighted that washing is a challenge for 30% of Roma because they live in households without tap water. Furthermore, up to 80% of Roma in some countries live in cramped Roma neighborhoods with overcrowded housing that makes physical distancing close to impossible. In addition, due to the level of poverty most Roma people are facing, buying medication, face masks and other forms of protective equipment is also a major challenge.

In terms of employment, many people lost their financial security and jobs and Roma are no exceptions. Those who often carry out low paid jobs depend on contact with other people or involve travel, such as collecting scrap material were unable to provide for their families during the quarantine.

FRA director Michael O'Flaherty said that 'already before the pandemic, many Member States failed to bring about real noticeable change for Europe's Roma communities.'

While all the then 28 EU member states have agreed to implement the 2011 EU Framework for National Roma Integration Strategies up to 2020 and its ambitious goals to close the gap between Roma and non-Roma in the key policy areas of education, employment, housing, and health as well as to protect Roma against discrimination, the pandemic brought its failure to light.

The initiative appeared to be groundbreaking at the time but due to its non-binding nature, the Framework left it to member states to decide the what and the how of the execution of their National Integration Strategies. As a result, many governments have not prioritised the allocation of sufficient funding or included robust monitoring.

The Open Society Foundation its 2019 report identified that the EU funds have failed to improve the lives of Roma due to lack of Roma participation; weak governance and coordination; lack of data on Roma; lack or robust monitoring of the spent funds; and lack of an anti-gypsyism approach.

it should not come as a surprise that police officers terrorising the communities in these unprecedented times continues to remain unchallenged, under reported and there is no interest in a collective public outcry to stand for the most persecuted minority group in Europe.

The last acceptable form of racism in Europe is against Roma. Police brutality has been a long-standing problem way before the pandemic, so it should not come as a surprise that police officers terrorising the communities in these unprecedented times continues to remain unchallenged, under reported and there is no interest in a collective public outcry to stand for the most persecuted minority group in Europe.

During the pandemic, video footage showed police officers in Romania beating eight handcuffed Roma men and one 13-year-old boy for allegedly having a barbeque outside one of their houses. Several policemen and gendarmes, in and out of uniform, took part in the collective punishment. Two officers were seen holding the arms of a Roma man screaming in agony, as a third whips the bare soles of his feet. Another officer was heard using racial slurs and threatened anyone who dared to report the incident.

In Slovakia, a police officer was beating and threatening to shoot a group of Roma children for allegedly breaking a military-imposed quarantine in the segregated Roma neighborhood.

However, incidents against Roma are not only the forte of Eastern Europe. In Belgium, families, including a pregnant woman and children, were evicted from their caravans by an armed team. In the Netherlands, officers used excessive force to arrest a Roma man and his two sons and pushing the mother of the family to the ground.

Being a Roma Rights advocate for the past decade makes me ask the question how could the world continue to cover up for centuries of anti-Roma law, medical experimentations on Roma people, forced sterilisation for decades, systemic segregation and institutional racism that oftentimes manifests in violence against Roma? It would be close to impossible to hold the communities accountable for the extreme poverty from the periphery, without seats around the decision-making table. Regardless, governments choose not to recognise the extreme level of mistreatment because to do so, that would lead to an international scandal. And there should be an international scandal to drastically change the current status quo of Roma communities in society. It is ought to be our collective responsibility to end anti-gypsism that is deeply rooted in our societal structures and has been exacerbated all the more by these recent global events.

Brigitta Balogh is a Roma rights advocate.

Marc Willers QC | COVID-19 hits black and ethnic minority people the hardest

When news of the spread of COVID-19 broke few of us could have imagined how badly our government would handle the pandemic in the coming months or what a devastating effect it would have on the lives of so many people and particularly those from black and minority ethnic (BAME) groups.

But it wasn't long after the lockdown was announced that I realised that the impact of the pandemic would exacerbate the difficulties already faced by some of the most vulnerable people in our society. The penny dropped when I was contacted by some of my existing Gypsy and Traveller clients who were being threatened with eviction from unauthorised encampments by local authorities despite the fact that they had nowhere else to go and would breach the government's lockdown if they were forced back onto the road, putting their health and that of others at risk. Fortunately, I was able to direct those clients to solicitors who were able to persuade the authorities to back off. But the very fact that the government had not placed a moratorium on such evictions seemed absurd and discriminatory, given its decision to prohibit evictions from housing during the pandemic. Many others held the same view and a number of NGOs wrote to the government to: highlight the fact that Gypsies and Travellers experience severe health inequalities and poor life outcomes and were consequently at an increased risk of severe illness from COVID-19; and call for a halt to all such evictions and the provision of access to water and sanitation for those living on unauthorised encampments.

Then another one of my clients informed me that two frontline BAME doctors working in the NHS were deeply concerned about the desperately short supply of personal protective equipment (PPE) for healthcare workers and wanted to take legal action to force the government to make proper provision of PPE for the protection of both their colleagues and their patients. Bindmans LLP were instructed and my Junior, Estelle Dehon, and I began reading the literature on PPE and the government's evolving guidance on its provision and use.

It was already abundantly clear that the government had failed to secure the supply of sufficient quantities of PPE, but that fact and the causes of its failure were matters that we considered would need to be addressed at an inquiry rather than in any claim for judicial review. After all, a judge couldn't order that the government supply PPE that it did not have.

Instead, we focussed on the government's claim that its guidance on the use of PPE by healthcare workers aligned with guidance issued by the World Health Organization (WHO). We concluded that there was a significant mismatch between the government's guidance and that issued by the WHO (which seemed to offer healthcare workers a greater level of protection) and that its guidance failed properly to warn healthcare workers of the risks they faced and their legal right to refuse to work when appropriate PPE is unavailable.

We also focussed on the fact that COVID-19 appeared to be having a grossly disproportionate impact on BAME healthcare workers. That fact was highlighted in an independent report by Cook, Kursumovic and Lennane which was published on 22 April 2020 and showed that 94% of the doctors and 71% of the nurses that had tragically died of COVID-19 by that time were from BAME backgrounds. The government ought to have been well aware of these shocking statistics yet it seemed that it had done little if anything to examine why BAME healthcare workers had been hit so hard by COVID-19 and that it had failed to take appropriate steps to mitigate the risks they faced.

Given that we are still in the midst of the COVID-19 pandemic with a very real risk of a second wave this coming winter, my clients felt they had no option but to issue a claim for judicial review and ask the court to declare that the government's PPE guidance is unlawful. They will also ask the court to order that it conducts an equality impact assessment on the effect of COVID-19 on BAME healthcare workers and revises its PPE guidance to mitigate that impact, so that those on the

Clapping for healthcare workers on a Thursday night showed we care for them but it is the provision of adequate PPE that will protect them from harm now and in the future.

frontline have adequate PPE which meets the WHO standards and BAME healthcare workers are properly protected.

Clapping for healthcare workers on a Thursday night showed we care for them but it is the provision of adequate PPE that will protect them from harm now and in the future.

Marc Willers QC, Garden Court Chambers.

Nicola Mackintosh QC (Hon) | Ensuring the hard-won rights of us all are not lost

In a time of universal deceit, telling the truth is a revolutionary act.

George Orwell

The word 'unprecedented' has never been used more often than now. For most, the relentless approach of the pandemic and its effect on how we relate to one another as human beings has been difficult to comprehend. For disabled people lacking capacity, including those with dementia or a learning disability, it has been catastrophic.

In the field of mental capacity and community care, we have seen a vast increase in numbers of disabled clients who are separated from their families, causing them intense distress. Many cannot process the logic of the need for physical separation from their loved ones and cannot understand why they are segregated and isolated. For many the use of technology is no solution as it merely emphasises the inability to have physical contact. It does not allow for the subtle nuances of non-verbal communication which are so vital.

There have been many accounts of the anguish of families being separated but for disabled people the distress and hardship is magnified. According to the Office for National Statistics, disabled people are significantly more likely to die of COVID-19 than the general population. This is not just due to underlying health conditions, but also decades of inequality in accessing services. And the illness, pain and in many cases death of people who most need family and loved ones with them is wholly incomprehensible.

We are seeing a worrying trend of further inequality of societal treatment of disabled people. And we have very serious concerns about the apparent overnight disposal of legal protections and safeguards for disabled people.

The decision to allow the formal suspension of duties under the Care Act 2014 by local authorities is illustrative of a dangerous road to removal or erosion of the rule of law for people lacking capacity or who are otherwise vulnerable. State agencies are under immense pressure, however the effective removal of established rights for people least able to protect themselves is unacceptable. Alongside the obvious deficits in the legal aid system which leaves the vast majority of the population without access to any legal advice or representation about even the most basic of needs – personal freedom and autonomy, access to food, healthcare, housing and contact with other human beings, and the situation is even more stark. And all of this is ironically at a time when people would be more likely to be safe in their own homes with packages of care than in residential or nursing care. Leaving people without proper advice means there is nowhere to turn. Rights and lives become worthless.

In relation to deprivation of liberty of people in care homes and hospitals the concern about the possible widespread reduction of fundamental rights and protections even prompted the Vice President of the Court of Protection, Mr Justice Hayden, to write to the Association of Directors of Social Services on 4 May 2020. He reminded them of their continuing obligations regarding detention of people lacking capacity thus:

> *The deprivation of the liberty of any individual in a democratic society, holding fast to the rule of law, will always require appropriate authorisation. Nothing has changed. The Mental Capacity Act 2005, the Court of Protection Rules and the fundamental rights and freedoms which underpin them are indispensable safeguards to the frail and vulnerable.*

Such a salutary reminder of fundamental rights is welcome but that it was considered necessary is a warning to us all. We must protect our rights and be ever vigilant about attempts to erode the rule of law still further.

There is no better barometer of the health of a society than

There is no better barometer of the health of a society than assessing how the most vulnerable people are treated and valued. We have a duty to keep a watchful eye on every dilution, and every removal of rights and protections, whether by process or substance or both, and to take action.

assessing how the most vulnerable people are treated and valued. We have a duty to keep a watchful eye on every dilution, and every removal of rights and protections, whether by process or substance or both, and to take action.

We must all tell the truth about what we see in order to hold to account those who wish to use this extraordinary event for other ends, intentionally or otherwise, so that the hard-won rights of us all are not lost.

Nicola Mackintosh QC (Hon) is co-director and founder of Mackintosh Law.

Zena Soormally Bolwig | Underfunding and disconnection in health and social care

I am a mental capacity and community care solicitor. I predominantly act in the Court of Protection, for individuals who cannot make decisions for themselves.

Most of my clients live in care homes or in the community with packages of care from the local authority or from the NHS. They often suffer as a result of unlawful, inappropriate or inadequate actions by the NHS or social care sector. Those actions are frequently the result of inadequate funding or lack of cohesion between those sectors.

Those injustices and routine failures pre-existed the pandemic, but this crisis has brought further hardship for my client group and has further marginalised them.

This pandemic has again shone a light on the disastrous consequences of continuing to undervalue and underfund our health and social care systems, and on the desperate need for health and social care to work more closely together.

First, there has been an immense loss of life in care homes. Nothing can justify it. According to recent reports, over half of the deaths during the pandemic are likely to be the result of deaths in care homes, and 25,000 people were discharged from hospitals to care homes during mid-March and mid-April, without being tested. The Government must take responsibility for its irresponsible communications, absent policies, lack of data in relation to hospital discharges and deaths, delayed lockdown, and inadequate testing during the initial stages of the pandemic. It did not prioritise the needs of, or manage the risks to, individuals in care homes or those being discharged to care homes. It simply did not do it, and thousands upon thousands of human beings have paid the highest price as a result.

In late March and April, the NHS was on the brink of collapse. I was an inpatient in a London hospital during the peak of COVID-19, thankfully for a non-COVID-19-related illness. There was panic about running out of ventilators and oxygen all over the ward, but to the outside world, you would never have known it. The only reason the NHS survived was due to the sacrifices made by those on the

51

The Government must take responsibility for its irresponsible communications, absent policies, lack of data in relation to hospital discharges and deaths, delayed lockdown, and inadequate testing during the initial stages of the pandemic.

frontline. It survived despite years of underfunding and clear failures of the Government to implement lockdown swiftly and to ensure sufficient provision of PPE for frontline workers.

There has been a disconnect between the NHS and social care historically. For example, clients are frequently told by local authorities that they cannot return to live in their homes following an acute admission, because the care they need cannot be provided safely there. Then, following a challenge within the Court of Protection, for example, an NHS Continuing Healthcare decision is made. Suddenly, that person, whose needs have not changed, can move home with a funded package of care. In those cases, if the two parts of the system worked more homogenously together, or if the balance of funding available to meet needs was equal between the NHS and social care, the client would have been protected and supported. The client could have, in those circumstances, lived at home many months, if not years, before and public money and time would have been saved.

The structure and funding of the health and care sector must be reviewed urgently. Our most vulnerable citizens simply cannot live with the respect and dignity they deserve and are entitled to if changes are not made. The public now see the unquestionable need for and benefit of a properly funded, cooperative and organised health and social care system. The lack of action, unclear messaging and opaque responses from the Government have exposed it to the inquisition of the nation; questions need to be answered and changes made.

The pandemic has been heart-breaking, life changing, and horrifying. Notwithstanding how dreadful it has been, we, as a profession, and as a country, have an opportunity now, and a platform on which we can fight for historic and ongoing inefficiencies and injustices to be remedied. We can build on the arguments above, and no doubt many more, to improve the lives of our clients, despite the tragedy many have faced.

Zena Soormally Bolwig is a solicitor and co-director of Mackintosh Law.

Tam Gill and Sophy Miles | Human contact is important

The coronavirus pandemic has impacted upon every aspect of life and existence for every person. For patients detained under the Mental Health Act 1983 (and 2007), it has pushed them into more polarised positions than ever before; those detained in hospital are struggling to achieve discharge as there are concerns around managing social isolation, a lack of face to face community follow up and a lack of clarity and motivation to procure and provide placement and funding.

For those in the community who require support, this support has been curtailed; some are able to access telephone or videolink input; others are not.

For those in the community requiring admission, it is a struggle for the relevant assessments under the Mental Health Act to take place; social distancing and lack of support (eg police, ambulance etc) precludes this at times, due to pressures from elsewhere within their roles and functions, and again due to concerns around social distancing.

Those detained under the Mental Health Act in hospital are at risk of infection, with mortality rates of detained patients doubling in 2020.

Those who escape COVID-19 are more isolated than before; not only is their liberty withheld, but social visits from family and friends has been stopped – some hospitals have arranged for virtual visits, but this is not across the board. Many hospitals have imposed blanket bans on section 17 leave, often a vital precursor to discharge. Our experience has been that, when this is challenged by solicitors for patients, some compromise is usually reached: but what of those who are not represented?

Treatments such as psychology, occupational therapy and other therapies (for example, music, drama, art) are either not available, or delivered via videolink facility; a poor second best, as the nuance and ability to open up and engage in therapy with a therapist is impaired by the presence of a video screen, and absence of a human being.

Human contact is important; its power cannot be underestimated. Lawyers may not be part of essential clinical staff, but often can be the un-heralded and informal member of the patient's multidisciplinary team; providing legal advice, assistance, resolving issues and at times, being able to speak frankly and objectively to patients about their care pathway and how they may wish to work towards their improved mental health and eventual discharge.

Peering at one's clinical team over a grainy videolink, barely able to hear what is being said; talking into a computer screen, not sure where to look; sitting in a room with many pairs of eyes focused on you and no ability to avoid the scrutiny – these are all issues that arise not only in clinical meetings for patients, but also in videolink hearings.

Whilst HM Courts & Tribunals Service is to be applauded for the speed at which the Cloud Video Platform (CVP) was implemented (First-tier Tribunal (Mental Health) being one of the trial courts for testing this system, which is now being rolled out into the Crown Courts), it is not without its drawbacks. The pre-hearing examination by the medical member can no longer take place. Hearings may take longer; advocacy becomes difficult, as the lawyer cannot use the non-verbal skills that often make the difference between a formulaic approach to a case, and a highly specialised, sensitive and client-centred approach that is imperative in the field of mental health law.

CVP is a more-than-adequate patch-fix (and certainly preferable to the telephone hearings that were used prior to its rollout), not a long-term solution. It should not become the 'new normal' post COVID-19 because of the disadvantages to the patient, for whom the tribunal itself exists.

Tam Gill is principal solicitor at Gledhill Gill Solicitors. Sophy Miles is a barrister at Doughty Street Chambers.

Steve Broach and Anne-Marie Irwin | Shining a light on disabled people's rights

The pandemic has exacerbated disabled people's experience of being left out of policy design, with predictable negative consequences for their rights and interests. At the time of writing, disabled people were expressing serious concern about the way the exemptions to the new requirement for face coverings on public transport were being ignored by politicians and the media.

Actual or threatened legal action has been repeatedly necessary to prevent indirect discrimination against disabled people arising from the pandemic. A striking instance of this was the challenge to the incorporation of the 'Clinical Frailty Scale' ('CFS') into the NICE guideline on access to critical care, which risked disabled people with high support needs being denied intensive care on the basis of a high 'frailty' score alone. NICE amended the guideline after receiving pre-action correspondence, but disabled people and their loved ones continued to fear the CFS would be used in practice. Two judicial reviews were intimated against the secretary of state for failing to issue clear guidance on how critical care should be prioritised in the event that demand outstripped supply, but in the event neither claim was issued. The NHS managed to avoid entering that 'rationing' scenario in relation to intensive care during the initial months of the pandemic, albeit at significant cost to other health services.

The pandemic also saw the continued and repeated misapplication of 'do not attempt cardiopulmonary resuscitation' notices to people with learning disabilities. This sense that disabled lives have less value than others was reinforced by the failure of relevant bodies to report an accurate total of the deaths of people with learning disabilities and/or autistic people during the pandemic. Again both of these issues have been subject to actual or threatened litigation.

The 'lockdown' also had a disproportionate adverse effect on disabled adults. Care homes and other settings began to impose blanket bans on visiting, failing to factor in the devastating impact these bans can have on the Article 8 ECHR rights of disabled residents. The government's 'lockdown' guidance went further than the regulations, in seeking to enforce a 'once a day' exercise restriction on people leaving home. This again had to be varied after the event, once a group of disabled people who needed to leave home to exercise more frequently to maintain their well-being threatened judicial review proceedings.

This sense that disabled lives have less value than others was reinforced by the failure of relevant bodies to report an accurate total of the deaths of people with learning disabilities and/or autistic people during the pandemic.

The legal issue affecting disabled adults which had the greatest amount of coverage turned out to be something of a damp squib. The Coronavirus Act 2020 cut a swathe through the entitlements to social care, including removing any duty to meet eligible needs under the Care Act 2014 in England unless to do so was necessary to avoid a breach of the ECHR. However, the secretary of state published statutory guidance which put in place a detailed and prescriptive process by which local authorities had to effectively bring these 'easements' into force.

This raised the spectre of a patchwork of local authorities, each applying different versions of adult social care law, making it impossible for legal advisers to support disabled people and their carers to access their entitlements. As it transpired, only eight local authorities have to date made the necessary decision to apply the 'easements' in their area, and at the time of writing (June 2020) only one local authority, Solihull, is doing so. The potential for wholesale disapplication of the Care Act duties has therefore not (yet) arisen. Though there is an obvious risk that further local authorities will adopt the 'easements' in the event of a second wave of cases.

One shard of light in relation to the pandemic has been the ability of disabled people and lawyers to respond quickly to arguably unlawful measures, often using crowdfunding to fill gaps in the legal aid scheme to allow judicial review claims to be threatened or promptly brought. The issues have also garnered significant media attention, shining a light on disabled people's rights in a way which is rarely seen under normal circumstances. It is likely that practitioners will continue to need to adopt this fleet footed approach to protecting and promoting disabled people's rights as we move into the next stage of the pandemic.

Steve Broach is a barrister at 39 Essex Chambers in London. Anne-Marie Irwin is partner at Rook Irwin Sweeney.

Steve Broach and Polly Sweeney | Already in crisis

The pandemic hit with the statutory system for children and young people with special educational needs and disabilities ('SEND') already in crisis. Countless reports from inspection bodies and parliamentary committees told the same story, of children and young people experiencing severe delays to get statutory assessments and plans, and routine failures to secure or arrange the education and health provision to which they eventually become entitled, if an Education, Health and Care (EHC) Plan is finally issued. Any promise from the reforms introduced through the Children and Families Act 2014 had long since dissipated.

And yet despite this bleak picture, the government in England decided that the appropriate response to the pandemic was to remove any enforceable duty to secure or arrange provision for children and young people with EHC Plans, and to relax almost all the timescales for the various steps in the EHC Plan process. The relaxation of timescales only arises where a 'coronavirus exception' applies, being when local authorities cannot reasonably take the required steps in the usual time for a coronavirus-related reason. But the reality is that local authorities were already routinely flouting these timescales in many cases well before the virus arrived, and it is fanciful to think that families are going to be in a position to unpick whether a local authority's delay has a genuine coronavirus-related cause in their case.

As families had to grapple with keeping the child or young person at home or relying on the 'vulnerable' exception and sending them to school, at the same time the government used powers given to it in the Coronavirus Act 2020 to downgrade the core duty in Children and Families Act 2014 s42, to secure and arrange education and health provision in EHC Plans, to a mere 'reasonable endeavours' duty. Unlike the timescale's relaxation under the Amendment Regulations, the change to the section 42 duties was not linked to individual case difficulties; it was a general undermining of a long-standing statutory duty which had provided a legal guarantee of appropriate provision for decades.

Not only was a Notice issued to downgrade the section 42 duties for May 2020, but a second Notice was issued achieving the same effect

The pandemic hit with the statutory system for children and young people with special educational needs and disabilities ('SEND') already in crisis.

for June 2020. In both cases, the Notices were issued at the very last minute, giving families, schools, colleges and other affected parties virtually no time to prepare for the significantly changed legal landscape. We can anticipate that any notice for July 2020 or subsequent months will again be issued at the last moment.

Both the May and June Notices and the Amendment Regulations have been challenged in a judicial review claim in which the authors of this piece are acting, instructed by two families with children with SEND. In this claim, the government has repeatedly asserted that a major trigger for the issuing of these instruments was the threat of legal action by families. At the time of writing (June 2020), the government has provided no evidence to show that any of these threats related to impossible or unreasonable demands from families. Both families bringing the judicial review claim are clear that they are not seeking to make local authorities do the impossible, and nor would any other family do so in their view. They are simply seeking to have the provision that their children need delivered, to the greatest possible extent that the pandemic allows. Unfortunately, the government's commitment to the rights of children and young people with SEND does not even extend this far.

Despite the statutory framework having been undermined in these significant ways, the ordinary business of tribunal appeals in relation to EHC Plans continues. The Tribunal has adapted well to the pandemic, being swift to introduce video hearings which seem to have had positive feedback overall. Whilst it is essential that any decision on the long-term use of remote hearings properly considers the views of litigants in person and the child or young person themselves, it seems that the pandemic has at least offered an opportunity to use technology to reduce the backlog in cases and is having a positive impact on the number of hearings needing to be adjourned.

Steve Broach is a barrister at 39 Essex Chambers in London. Polly Sweeney is partner at Rook Irwin Sweeney.

Celia Kitzinger and Gill Loomes-Quinn | Remote justice and transparency in the post-lockdown Court of Protection

On 15 June 2020, in the midst of the global health emergency, we launched the Open Justice Court of Protection Project. Its aim is to promote Open Justice in the Court of Protection (COP) by supporting the public to observe hearings, and publishing observations and other reflective blogs on our website. We have been supported by the judiciary and in particular the HIVE group (established by the Vice President of the COP to support its work throughout the COVID-19 health crisis) which laid out from the start of the pandemic its commitment to ensuring that 'the considerable efforts made to achieve a properly transparent Court of Protection are not undermined by the exigencies of the social distancing imperative'.

The COP was established in its current form in 2007, by the Mental Capacity Act 2005. It makes decisions on financial and welfare matters for people deemed not to have capacity to make those decisions due to an 'impairment of, or disturbance in the functioning of the mind or brain' (eg dementia, autism or brain injury). The court profoundly impacts disabled people – both the individuals at the centre of its decisions (eg in making decisions about where they live, or whether they receive certain medical treatments) and, through its published judgments, disabled people, their families, friends, and professional supporters far beyond its walls. Initially, most hearings were private – except 'serious medical treatment' cases (eg decisions about life-sustaining treatments or sterilisation) – but since 2016 when the Court of Protection Transparency Pilot was launched, most hearings have been in public – with generally poor attendance.

Gill was among the first researchers to use the Transparency Pilot to access the Court of Protection as a Public Observer; observing 14 hearings in February 2017. Celia had observed around two dozen hearings between late 2011 and March 2020 – all concerning serious medical treatment – as part of her work supporting families via the Coma and Disorders of Consciousness Research Centre. Then, on 17 March 2020, less than 24 hours after the Prime Minister's announcement to the nation to avoid all non-essential contact due to

COVID-19, she attended the first all-remote hearing. While much of the legal profession at the time celebrated the swift move to video-platforms and telephone conferencing, Celia raised serious concerns about the impact on lay participants. This was a catalyst for further research and advocacy that led to the inception of the Open Justice Court of Protection Project to promote public scrutiny of the court. The public health crisis enabled public access remotely, without the need to travel – via phone or laptop from home.

Our project has now existed for five weeks. In this short time, we have created an information resource for public observers via our website; addressing concerns and knowledge gaps impeding public access to COP hearings – eg how to request access to hearings, what a Transparency Order means, and how to behave in (virtual) court. We have also established short-term partnerships (eg with Essex Law School and with social workers in Herefordshire's Service Transformation Team). Our single biggest ongoing task involves collating and publicising details of COP hearings from existing list-ings (around 30 hearings per day). This involves hours of scrolling through CourtServe (as well as the First Avenue House and Family Division lists) searching out COP hearings, and contact email addresses and phone numbers (which are rarely provided!) so the public can request access. This is tedious and complicated – made more so by the fact that COP hearings are often not designated as such, and are equally like to appear on 'family' and 'civil' lists.

We cannot know how many people have observed hearings through our project, but we hear from lawyers that it has become common to have an observer in court; and we have personally attended hearings with between 10 and 15 public observers each. These have been largely health and social care staff, lawyers, and family members of people lacking capacity (including some with forthcoming COP hearings concerning their family member).

The move to online platforms, triggered by the COVID-19 pandemic, risked excluding the public from COP hearings; but instead, it has offered unprecedented access. In the short time since we established the project, we have discovered a considerable public appetite for engagement with the work of the COP. Professionals in various sectors (health, social care, law, voluntary sector) recognise oppor-tunities to develop their practice; and disability rights campaigners want to bear witness to the impact of the court on their communities.

We want the progress made in these challenging times to be driven forward in a post-lockdown world. There are complexities to be ironed out – enhancing the opportunities for some groups, while addressing the barriers created for others;

We want the progress made in these challenging times to be driven forward in a post-lockdown world.

but there are straightforward gains available too. We suggest the single biggest improvement to meaningful public engagement with the COP would be achieved by publication of a consolidated list of hearings – properly annotated with details such as the impairments of P, and the issues to be discussed. Only with access to such information are professionals and activists able to schedule the time to observe a hearing about issues relevant to their work.

We know Open Justice comes at a cost: ensuring hearings are publicly accessible, while maintaining the privacy and dignity of those at the centre of a hearing, demands time, effort, and skill of legal professionals and court staff. But our experience shows that for those whose professional and personal lives are touched by the work of the COP, Open Justice is an idea whose time has come. The development of technological infrastructure to maintain public access post-Lockdown will justify such costs by making transparency in the COP a reality.

Celia Kitzinger and Gill Loomes-Quinn are co-directors of the Open Justice Court of Protection Project.

Karen Buck MP | The crisis of un-met housing need

It is, of course, always the hope that destroys you. My constituents hope so very much that I can help them with the desperate problems they bring to me. I live in hope that the sheer illogicality of the way we meet housing needs will trigger a fundamental rethink of policy, even where the obvious misery it causes does not. In the exceptionally fraught weeks through of spring and early summer, I hoped even more that we would recognise we could not go back to the way we were, that lessons would at last be learned. Well, we will see.

COVID-19 and the ensuing lockdown brutally exposed what was already well known to practitioners. That is, we have a series of inter-locking crises of unmet housing need that traps those with the least market power in the worst housing conditions, or with no settled housing provision at all, facing lacking security and increasingly without access to the advice and representation that might help them. We knew already that bad housing – whether it is manifested via homelessness or disrepair – has huge consequences for people's health and for NHS spending. The pandemic has laid that bare. As work done by *Inside Housing* reveals in a series of stark charts, over-crowding, high levels of housing in multiple occupations and home-lessness are all correlated with some of the highest concentrations of COVID-19 mortality. Correlation is not causation, of course, and we know that bad or inappropriate housing is itself a proxy of wider social and economic disadvantage, but equally we can be confident that action on various housing fronts can help us turn those inequal-ities around. At the same time, what became newly obvious is that in a world changed fundamentally by the pandemic, other people's bad housing potentially has consequences for the rest of us. The easy spread of a disease with a high fatality rate and as yet no cure should be focusing government minds on housing solutions.

Of course, some valuable, albeit temporary, measures did indeed get put into place in the spring, demonstrating very clearly that where there is a will there is a way. Most visibly, the 'Everybody In' initiative saw the large majority of our street homeless population accommod-ated within days. In my own borough, the sudden vacating of cheaper tourist hotels created an opportunity to put a roof over people's heads and intensify the personal support many homeless people with complex needs require. After having seen rough sleeping double in a decade, we had, and have, a rare opportunity to turn a crisis measure into a lasting solution. The first 'late lockdown' signs weren't as encouraging as they might have been, as the hotel bookings looked like they would end

I live in hope that the sheer illogicality of the way we meet housing needs will trigger a fundamental rethink of policy, even where the obvious misery it causes does not.

before alternative provision was in place but an announcement in the last days of June extended the funding again, allowing some much-needed time. Welcome, too, were the suspension of evictions, inevitable, though only conceded after much pressure. This too has been given a further extension till August (a pattern is emerging here . . .). Critically, there was also some additional relief for those on low incomes, via Universal Credit, Local Housing Allowance and local authority Discretionary Housing and Local Payments.

Yet although we can be thankful that we haven't faced a summer of soaring homelessness (and it would have happened – one recent email to me from a landlord bemoaned the fact that they couldn't go ahead with evicting a mother and autistic child 'who clearly only wanted a council flat'), the underlying problems remain. The economic storm front is already upon us, with job losses, falling earnings and soaring debts. Poorer households on legacy benefits have lost out on the extra help given to Universal Credit claimants, and the two-child limit and benefit cap remain in place. There's every likelihood that homelessness will soar when the evictions ban is lifted, and noises have come from government indicating a lessening of enthusiasm for the promised ending of section 21.

There are certainly no signs of a renaissance of social housing, as called for (cross-party) by the Local Government Association. For alongside any rise in homelessness, we still have all those people in overcrowded homes, like the two health care workers in my constituency who share a one-bed flat with their two children. All those people in temporary accommodation, often stranded far from their support networks. All those in unfit homes, like those of my constituents who call in almost daily with damp, collapsed ceilings, pest infestations. All those paying half, or two thirds, of their net income for a room or two, or sofa surfing and never being quite sure where they may be bedding down from one night to the next. Meg Hillier, Chair of Parliament's Public Accounts Committee, and I have proposed to government an emergency housing package that makes use of unsold new build homes to relieve some of these pressures. Such a housing rescue package formed part of the response to the post-recession homelessness crisis of 1990 and could play a part now. We are hoping for a positive response from government. It's always the hope . . .

Karen Buck is member of parliament for Westminster North.

Giles Peaker | All too fragile

The rapid lesson about our housing system and the courts in dealing with housing matters from the pandemic was how hugely fragile it all is. We knew, of course, that there has been a developing housing crisis over many years, with an acute shortage of affordable rented accommodation and property prices based on a model of property ownership as financial asset rather than homes. We knew that the courts were under-funded, under-staffed, and creaking along on goodwill and unpaid work. But when the lockdown hit, it became rapidly apparent that there was no resilience in either system at all.

In the face of what looked like an imminent rapid rise in the number of rent arrears possession claims, in the middle of the pandemic, the government moved spasmodically from exhorting landlords to be nice, to extending notice periods for notices seeking possession, to asking the judiciary to impose a complete stay on possession proceedings.

This last, the stay, was also a response to what was rapidly becoming a chaotic situation in the county courts. The usual possession lists of 10 or 12 cases per court per morning or afternoon continued in the early days of the lockdown, despite the utter inability of the court estate to provide safe distancing for court staff, judges, parties or legal representatives. Waiting rooms filled with people, and unwell people turning up because their home was at risk, was a week or two of madness.

There were other issues. Some reports suggest illegal evictions rose, at the more criminal end of the rented sector. Repairs all but stopped, leaving some tenants enduring terrible conditions, but landlords arguing there was nothing they could do about it.

There were some positives. As the hotels and 'Airbnb lets' stood empty, it suddenly turned out that it was possible to end most street homelessness, as the government realised that thousands of people sleeping rough during the pandemic was not a good idea, regardless of any statutory priority need.

The trouble is, at the time of writing, that nobody knows what happens next. There are some indicators, and they are not encouraging.

The funding to accommodate the street homeless has been ended. While some Government funds have been brought forward by a year or two for supported housing, the amount is not sufficient to enable all those who were temporarily housed to move into lasting accommodation. Some, perhaps many, will be back into street homelessness.

The stay on possession cases, now extended to 23 August 2020, has no off-ramp. All that the Government has committed to is a 'pre-action protocol' that would extend to private landlords. Presumably this will be modelled on the current social landlords possession pre-action protocol, setting out duties to contact the tenant, to under-stand their situation and to seek to come to arrangements on repayment of arrears.

If that is all the Government proposes, it will not be enough. It would do nothing to prevent or avoid section 21 possession claims, where no ground is needed and possession is mandatory, nor mandatory Ground 8 rent arrears possession claims.

There may be a certain irony in that what may slow the likely wave of possession claims once the stay is lifted, and afterwards as the likely economic impact of the lockdown takes effect, is the state of the county courts. There is a large backlog of possession cases already, and it is growing fast. But the traditional means of dispatching possession claims – the possession lists days – will not be possible for many months, if ever again.

But the courts, at the time of writing, don't know how they will deal with housing cases. There were some early suggestions that hearings would be by phone or video only, despite this being practically inaccessible for many tenants, who could not access electronic bundles, file documents, or have the equipment or phone credit to attend virtually. And of course, there would be no duty scheme advice, making for an access to justice disaster.

Too few judges, too few courts, too few legal aid lawyers. It was all too fragile, and the coming months and years may show it is all broken.

We don't yet know what will finally be proposed. But

whatever it is in the 'new normal' will test justice to its limits for tenants and delay possession proceedings. Too few judges, too few courts, too few legal aid lawyers.

It was all too fragile, and the coming months and years may show it is all broken.

Giles Peaker is a partner at Anthony Gold Solicitors.

Nick Bano | What should possession law look like?

RENT

For as long as it has existed, housing law has been based on two assumptions. The first is that tenant households generally can, and generally will, pay their rent. The second is that – if they don't – it's fair enough that landlords should be able to evict them.

One of the consequences of coronavirus, however, is that the first assumption no longer holds true.

In many parts of the housing-crisis-ridden UK, housing costs were already pushing the boundaries of people's means before the pandemic hit. Rents were barely affordable. But a huge number of people are about to see a very sudden and significant drop in their incomes. Incomes at a society-wide level will fall very quickly (i.e. before rental markets can adjust), which is likely to mean that an unprecedented proportion of households will unable to afford their rent and unable to repay the arrears.

This means that rent arrears will no longer be the misfortune of a marginal number of households, but will instead become a broad social phenomenon.

If the first assumption is no longer correct, can the second assumption be maintained?

The idea that people can and should be evicted for rent arrears is surely unsuitable for a society where rent arrears are rife instead of exceptional. That is particularly true where there is a very serious pre-existing housing and homelessness crisis. Mass evictions and homelessness, in the context of a severe shortage of housing supply, is surely a disastrous backdrop for a society that will need to recover from the social and economic consequences of a deadly pandemic.

Legislators and commentators have struggled with this issue. The government has adopted an ineffective 'prevention is better than cure' approach of (temporarily, and probably unsustainably) bolstering wages and increasing the rates of housing benefit. There is also fairly broad support for the idea of suspending the mandatory rent arrears grounds for possession and abolishing section 21. But perhaps, instead of tinkering with the variables of the existing housing law framework, it has become necessary to look at the fundamental principles.

We will need to loosen the connection between rent arrears and evictions. Society can no longer operate on the basis that the existence of arrears makes it very likely that households will be evicted, or we risk compounding a homelessness crisis that was already intolerable. This means that we need to re-frame or replace the grounds for possession, tailoring them for a post-covid society.

Mass evictions and homelessness, in the context of a severe shortage of housing supply, is surely a disastrous backdrop for a society that will need to recover from the social and economic consequences of a deadly pandemic.

If we were to start again, and re-draw the essential principles of housing law for a society recovering from the pandemic, what should possession law look like?

One idea, though there are bound to be many others, is to replace all of the grounds for possession by re-introducing the old land law concept of 'greater hardship'. This simple test would force the courts to address the overall fairness of the outcome of evictions cases, instead of focussing on the money. This is a much more appropriate approach to evictions for a society where arrears are commonplace, and where housing is in short supply.

How would this work in practice? Suppose a tenant loses her job and accrues two or three months' arrears. She has no prospect of repaying the arrears any time soon, but she can pay the rent – or at least most of it. Her landlord owns two or three rental properties. Under the existing framework (even if ground 8 is abolished) the court is very likely to evict her: it would be reasonable to make a possession order, and it would not be reasonable to suspend it. The court's hands are tied. But if the landlord had to show greater hardship, the same tenant probably wouldn't be evicted. It would be a stretch for the landlord to show that their own circumstances outweighed the tenant's, and the court would have much more freedom to achieve a just outcome.

The courts might also be empowered to impose conditions on any possession order: they could order tenants to repay arrears, but at a rate that would not cause more hardship than an eviction would cause.

'Greater hardship' is also a fair replacement for anti-social behaviour grounds. The court could look at the hardship that a tenant has caused to their neighbours and weigh up the competing needs and interests.

Housing law no longer reflects society's needs. The grounds for possession were framed under very different circumstances and are no longer appropriate. Bold proposals are necessary to ensure that society is adequately housed as we recover from the pandemic.

Nick Bano is a social welfare law barrister at Garden Court Chambers.

Izzy Köksal | Collectivising our individual housing problems

Together we are stronger. We believe that with mutual support, collective action and solidarity, those at the worst end of the housing crisis can create the social change and justice we desperately need. Housing Action Southwark and Lambeth ('HASL') is a group of families and individuals struggling with homelessness and poor housing conditions. We support each other with our cases and fight for high quality, safe, secure council homes we all need.

Over the last three years, our meetings often had more than 100 people with immediate housing issues. Large group meetings are at the core of what we do and is how we facilitate collective support and action on housing and other poverty problems with our members. Breaking into smaller groups, we talk about our housing issues and share experiences, rights information and support. As common problems emerge, we build campaigns to challenge the root causes of our issues and try to bring about wider change.

Collectivising our individual housing problems is powerful in many ways. We give and receive support from the group, and we experience winning together. People bring food to share and the warmth and victory celebrations create a party atmosphere. Fowsiyo's, one of our member's, children call our meetings the 'parents' party' and would ask to miss school to come along.

We know that we are stronger together: as a source of energy, determination, comfort, company, friendship, and knowledge. This is housing organising and solidarity in action with people directly affected taking the lead and running the show. These meetings are the opposite of social distancing as we huddle together as more and more people try to squeeze into our hall.

With COVID-19 the meetings have had to stop but our tactics of mutual support and collective action remain the same. We have been adapting by trying to organise collective support and action remotely with Zoom, we have had tours of flats – sho wing disrepair and over-

We know that we are stronger together: as a source of energy, determination, comfort, company, friendship, and knowledge.

crowded conditions and we have started a postcard protest for one family. We delivered postcards across south London to HASL members and received over 100 photos of HASL members and supporters which we uploaded onto Twitter. Many of the people in the photos are also living in overcrowded homes or have done so in the past. We were able to show that we are still here for each other despite not being able to meet physically. It has been really moving and inspiring to see so many familiar faces and the energy with which people responded to the request.

But while it has been a good way to stay in contact, there are lots of important aspects of physical meetings that it cannot replace – enabling families to escape overcrowded homes (albeit to an over-crowded hall), dedicated children's activities, sharing food, and other conversations and socialising during and after meetings. Nothing can replace the cheer of over one hundred people when a family announce they have moved into a new council home.

Members have contacted us saying they hope we can meet again soon but it feels very hard to imagine, not just in terms of our cramped meeting hall, but so many of our members have many of the underlying factors making them particularly at risk of COVID-19.

Throughout the pandemic, and the additional hardship it has caused, we have kept in contact and also welcomed new members to the group. Talking about housing and other concerns and difficulties we are facing, reminding people that they are not alone and finding ways to help each other. We've also developed stronger links with many of our sister grassroots groups and housing lawyers across London, joining and supporting each other's projects and campaigns. With each of our hard-fought victories, we have been inspired by the power of collective action.

During the pandemic we saw what we knew and believed: it really is so simple to end evictions, end benefit sanctions, increase benefits, release people from immigration detention, and make sure everyone has housing. Many of these things were achieved by dedicated campaigning, legal challenges, and public pressure. There is still so much more that needs to be done but these policies are proof that demands that previously might have been viewed as radical are actually just common sense – and that they are possible right now.

But, as soon as these changes were brought in the government was looking for a way out, which is why grassroots organising and campaigns are needed more than ever to create a society without poverty, homelessness, and injustice.

Izzy Köksal is a member of Housing Action Southwark and Lambeth.

Tom Royston | Making our benefits system work for us all

The UK government's response to the effects of COVID-19 emergency on workers' incomes reflected a national consensus that we should support each other in hard times. The fact that its response required not just more *money*, but also the suspension or alteration of major parts of social security *law*, illuminated that our benefits system does not, at the moment, successfully reflect that consensus. We should not waste that lesson.

What we need is a benefit system which helps us live a dignified and decent life in the face of economic misfortune and does not exclude any part of our society from its safety net.

Benefit rates, conditionality and dignity

The blanket suspension of the sanctions regime and the minimum income floor would not have been necessary if those measures had, in the first place, been sufficiently well designed to respond humanely to the wide range of difficulties which can befall a household.

Likewise the creation of a 'furlough' wage support scheme, the self-employed income support scheme, and the temporary boost to Universal Credit, all attempting to secure a civilised level of household income for temporarily inactive workers, would have been unnecessary if the level of benefit entitlement which we tolerate in this country (both for means tested and contributory benefits) were not set at rates which produce widespread and undignified poverty.

John Veit-Wilson grounded both those issues in principles of basic human rights:

> Human rights conventions refer to a dignified and decent level of living. That means having freedom to choose to live a socially inclusive life, to do all the same silly, wasteful things that everyone else can do, whatever their personal problems, without themselves becoming poor. It means not being told how to live your life by other people who control your resources.

As we emerge from this period of economic disruption, his reasoning ought to inform the decisions being made about the structure and operation of the welfare state. The lesson may be that provisions which do not work in a crisis do not, in fact, work at other times either.

Children are people

What we need is a benefit system which helps us live a dignified and decent life in the face of economic misfortune and does not exclude any part of our society from its safety net.

Footballer Marcus Rashford's account of growing up hungry prompted the government to temporarily extend access to free school meals in summer 2020. But as his powerful letter to MPs pointed out, a significant part of the problem is the rupture in the historic link between need and provision in the benefits system, particularly where it comes to children. Most obviously, the 'two-child limit' on benefits means children in large families – whether or not their parents work – are excluded from the social security safety net, making hopelessly inadequate the per capita amounts those families are expected to live on. Summer school meal vouchers cannot remedy that problem. The adult-focussed nature of the furlough and self employment schemes, and the temporary increase in Universal Credit rates for adults, suggest that child rights have not been a top crisis response priority for social security policymakers.

The next few years are likely to see many families in economic hardship which they could not reasonably have foreseen at the time of any decisions about how many children to have. And nobody would suggest the children of large families can reasonably be held responsible for their own hunger. At the same time, many citizens will be hoping that our political leaders will try to strengthen the sense of community cohesion which might have been the sole positive feature of the 2020 public health emergency. One way to do that would be to ensure that everyone – whether adult or child, and regardless of the number of their siblings – is allowed to participate in the system of mutual support which social security exists to provide.

Tom Royston is a barrister at Garden Court North Chambers.

David Renton | In protecting jobs, you save people's homes

One of the lessons of the crisis is the connectedness of employment and housing. Early on in the lockdown, it became clear that millions of workers were employed on contracts which their employers regarded as impermanent, and capable of being terminated at will. Many employers simply declared themselves insolvent; while others, even though they continued, to trade, simply opted out of all employment protections.

Around two million people made Universal Credit claims in the first six weeks of the lockdown. For each of those dismissed, the loss of employment was a disaster: they had less money; but they still have to pay all their existing debts.

Research conducted by Britain's 187 district councils, estimates that before the lockdown struck more than 480,000 families in Britain were living in private housing and paying more than half their total income in rent. Each of them was at risk of eviction.

A survey by HouseMark suggested that social housing tenants were also in danger: total social housing debt, it estimated, rose by £100 million in the first six weeks of the lockdown, with total rental income falling by 3 percent in a month.

Moreover, with each job that was lost, money drained out of the economy. Because workers had been dismissed and were not receiving wages, so they spent less, and the demand for other businesses fell. The loss of one job led to the loss of another until it was hardly possible to imagine how anything like the old economy could be restored.

Two lessons I take from Coronavirus are that we need to pay keyworkers more, and we need to protect everyone better against unemployment.

With regards to pay: during the lockdown, society depended on nurses, delivery drivers and transport workers. Schools were required to educate their children, even while the rest of us stayed at home. But this definition of key work was utterly at odds with the normal way in which we structure reward. Shelf stackers working in chemists and supermarkets turned out to be absolutely essential; while all number of high-income people: marketing staff, financial planners and chief executives, stayed at home.

The Living Wage Foundation estimates that a single person needs to be paid £10.75 an hour in London or £9.30 an hour

The loss of one job led to the loss of another until it was hardly possible to imagine how anything like the old economy could be restored.

outside to pay for food, clothing and bills. It turns out that 92 percent of shelf-fillers, 73 percent of dispensing assistants in pharmacies, and 60 percent of nursery nurses, don't earn enough to live.

In Britain until the mid-1980s pay was kept through negotiations between unions and employer's organisations, setting wage rates for each sector of the economy. In 1979, four-fifths of all workers' terms and conditions were subject to collective bargaining, now, that figure has fallen to just one in five (the European average is over 60 percent). The collapse of these structures has been good news for employers; but it has been disastrous in those parts of the economy where pay is low, turnover high, and which are almost impossible to organise without the state requiring proper negotiations.

Second, during the lockdown, millions of workers lost their jobs. Where staff were dismissed, they had a degree of protection: redundancy payments are protected by the state where a company is insolvent. The cruellest cases were the ones where ostensibly there was no dismissal. Zero-hour contracts workers were told they remained on the employer's books but would be given no work. Self-employed contracts were simply cancelled and, not being employees, such workers had no protection against dismissal.

The evil of zero-hour contracts could be reformed away by allowing for variable hour contracts but insisting they had a minimum content: say, 14 hours a week.

As for self-employment, the proportion of employees who are categorised as self-employed has doubled in the past forty years. In a tiny number of cases, this has been due to the expansion of occupations which are genuinely self-employed: a medical consultant offering her services to a group of private sector hospitals is a business, trading equally in relation to the companies who engage her. You could say the same about barristers.

Far more common though is bogus self-employment, as is now prevalent in construction, where workers are required to set up formal business as the price of securing work. If you want to know why building sites kept open during COVID-19 while offices didn't, it's because of this self-employment: the owners wanted to keep sites open, and the workers reluctantly agreed – if they didn't work, they wouldn't be paid. In keeping the sites open, the builders' lives were put at risk for the sake of company profits.

In a fairer system, self-employment would be restricted to a tiny number of genuine self-employees, while all other workers and employees should be in a single category of 'worker' with full access to the minimum wage and unfair dismissal rights.

Such a system would be of material advantage to the workers affected: they would be secure in their employment and protected against dismissal. But it would also be of benefit to others as well: landlords would be better protected, if their workers were confident in the knowledge that their employment was secure. And taxpayers too would be shielded: the cost of keeping workers in their homes would be on their employers, rather than falling on general taxation and on everyone.

David Renton is a barrister at Garden Court Chambers.

Zachary Whyte | The horror of the crisis has galvanised the legal community to find its feet and fight

Legal Sector Workers United ('LSWU') is a branch of the trade union United Voices of the World ('UVW'). It was founded in April 2019 to fight for legal sector workers to be properly compensated, fairly treated and secure in their job. As well as this, the union ambitiously campaigns for access to justice to be restored and extended. In order to make this objective a reality, we seek to become the union of the sector.

COVID-19 has led to a surge in small and large scale industrial battles across the legal sector. Workers being discriminated against, workers fired where they should be made redundant, workers being made redundant where they could have been furloughed, those shielding being refused furlough, pay being unilaterally cut – the list is long. Workplaces are adapting to this new reality and some employers have been far better than others. LSWU exists to combat those employers who have fallen short of the standards we expect in workplaces across the Britain and Ireland through organising within and between workplaces and bringing legal challenges.

We are seeing and grappling with the government's total disregard for legal workers. In the criminal justice sector for instance, no arrangements were put in place for police station attendance. LSWU intervened, pushing for the creation of the Police Station Protocol which keeps police station representatives safe through making remote access attendances possible. The courts have been left haphazardly open and we have seen chaos in magistrates' courts, with many cases being unnecessarily listed for the same time and a proposing to extend court hours further (after having sold off many of the criminal courts which has been a key factor in causing this backlog). LSWU supports the #strike4justice campaign that has developed around the issues facing criminal practitioners.

One of the next challenges LSWU anticipates is the return to offices for many of our members. With the government appearing to bring lockdown to an end we are seeing firms begin to direct their workers back to the office. This raises safety concerns and LSWU took a strong stance since before the announcement of the March lockdown that workers should be free to work from home. It's easy to forget the risk of the pandemic if those close to you aren't affected and life is seemingly continuing as normal, but the risk of serious harm remains real.

During a global pandemic, employers falling below the expected standards has the effect of exposing workers to serious health risks and even death. The union has managed to bring about huge changes within individual workplaces and in the words of one of our members: 'It's amazing how real and tangible the power of people united can be – I think everyone feels the energy! The sense of trust, cooperation and honesty this process has created is quite incredible'. By bringing together colleagues, creating a space for worker-led discussion, formulating action points and acting upon them we have proven that workers are the force for improving their working conditions.

Class consciousness has been raised and people are seeing that if they want their voices heard they need to collectivise.

The fast-moving situation across the country has led to a resurgence in the trade union movement. Within our sector union membership has more than tripled since the outbreak. Class consciousness has been raised and people are seeing that if they want their voices heard they need to collectivise. Collective action does not only play out in the workplace but spills out into the wider world. LSWU is a campaigning union with a view to improving the sector overall, and this includes major issues like restoring the legal aid budget and opposing systemic racism within our legal system.

During the pandemic we have forced employers to implement work from home policies and top up furlough pay, overturned redundancy decisions and challenged the legality of mass redundancies. The members of LSWU have fought for the Police Station Protocol to be adopted, for release from detention for all those held in immigration detention during the pandemic, for BPTC student's voices on discriminatory assessments to be heard through the SABER campaign, for exposure of the systemic racism of the legal sector via the #LawSoWhite campaign and much more.

82

Democracy and transparency is at the heart of LSWU and since lockdown the branch has taken time to elect a new committee and improve channels of communication and accountability within the organisation. As well as enjoying UVW's casework and legal support, LSWU has established its own casework team to assist individual members, these are employment law volunteers: members helping members, and suing employers for tens of thousands of pounds. An organising team was also established and we are forging ahead with plans to create a 'representatives committee' where elected union representatives from our various workplaces will sit.

LSWU has acted as an incubator for the sector's most radical campaigns. A members-led, fighting trade union is pivotal at this critical period where austerity looms and an economic crisis is likely to follow. We've skilled up on organising through reading groups, practice and guidance from our overarching union.

LSWU is ready to take on what challenges follow.

Zachary Whyte is a co-ordinator for Legal Sector Workers United (LSWU).

Rosalind Bragg | Safety for all women, without exception

From the beginning of the pandemic, pregnant women have struggled to negotiate safe working conditions. Pregnant care workers are expected to work with patients with COVID-19 symptoms, often with inadequate Personal Protective Equipment (PPE). Women working in smaller supermarkets are directed to remain on the tills, even where social distancing is not in place. Key workers are placed under enormous pressure to continue working in front line roles and in busy office environments.

The law requires employers to offer pregnant women safe working conditions or else suspension on full pay. In practice, many women who question workplace safety are given a choice between badly paid sick leave or unpaid leave. Despite declaring pregnant women to be a 'vulnerable group', the Government has not released guidance on health and safety for pregnant women. As a direct result of this omission, large numbers of employers are failing to meet their obligations to pregnant workers and pregnant women have been left distressed and anxious. Even women armed with legal advice are being refused their entitlements.

Financial pressures force many women to continue working in unsafe roles. Migrant women with no recourse to public funds face greater pressure as they are ineligible for Universal Credit and other benefits. Women on zero hours contracts, agency workers and casual workers have very weak health and safety protections. Pregnant women who have worked for the same employer for years are being told to go home and apply for Universal Credit, as their insecure contract gives them no right to suspension on full pay. The financial impacts extend into the maternity leave period, as maternity pay entitlements are dependent on income during pregnancy.

Furlough provisions, contained in the Coronavirus Job Retention Scheme, should have helped employers to place pregnant women on well-paid leave, and some did take advantage of the scheme. Many employers didn't do so, believing that pregnant women were ineligible. Their confusion was understandable, as the Government did not mention pregnant women in the guidance. Despite repeated requests to provide clarification, including a series of Parliamentary Questions, the Government has not amended the guidance to address this.

Lifting lockdown provisions before resolving school and childcare provision has created new problems for employed mothers. The Prime Minister has called for employers to be understanding but has provided no protections for women whose employers are not flexible. Women returning from maternity leave who can't organise childcare are being told to resign.

The Government's current 'hands-off' approach to pregnant women in the workplace threatens to wind back progress on gender equality, reducing women's economic independence and increasing the gender pay gap.

The Government's current 'hands-off' approach to pregnant women in the workplace threatens to wind back progress on gender equality, reducing women's economic independence and increasing the gender pay gap. Even before the pandemic, there was already ample evidence that mothers regularly face unfair and unlawful treatment at work. Research from 2016 found that 11% of pregnant women and new mothers in the workplace lost their jobs because of discrimination (EHRC, 2016).

Socio-economic inequalities and inequalities in health outcomes are becoming further entrenched. BAME women are more likely to be in insecure employment (TUC, 2017) and in public facing roles, increasing the risk of workplace infection. BAME women also face significantly higher maternal mortality rates than the rest of the population (MBRRACE-UK 2019). Hostile environment policies which exclude women from benefits and service based on their immigration status leave women in poverty and destitution. It is not possible for pregnant women to practice social distancing in overcrowded accommodation or while 'sofa surfing'.

Protecting the health and well-being of pregnant women in a pandemic, and at any other time, means women having safe, secure employment and universal access to Social Security. We need

Government to intervene to place strict limits on insecure employment contracts, to inspect and enforce workplace health and safety, to provide greater protection against unfair redundancy, and to protect the jobs of parents balancing work and care. We need a Social Security system which is available to all women, without exception, and which allows pregnant women, new mothers and their families to live dignified and healthy lives.

Rosalind Bragg is director of Maternity Action UK.

Audrey Ludwig | Watch this space

There is such a volume of material on unlawful discrimination issues arising from COVID-19 and the lockdown that this piece will only scrape the surface. Pre-pandemic there were already problems in discrimination law and practice including:

- difficulty for ordinary people in enforcing rights due to complexity and cost;
- long delays in bringing claims both in employment tribunals and county courts;
- the lack of expertise in county court judges in trying discrimination cases leading to calls for a combined Employment and Equality Court;
- the low numbers of legal aid certificates granted by the Legal Aid Agency and the scarcity of specialist lawyers.

The delays will be exacerbated by lockdown as discrimination claims are lengthy and complex and ill-suited to remote hearings. New issues are also coming to the fore. Many protected classes have been adversely impacted and we are already hearing of planned legal action.

Analysis by University College London has found BAME people are two or three times more likely to die from COVID-19 than the general population. This raises concern about workplace policies that adversely affect people who work in potentially unsafe workplaces or who are being made redundant because they are unwilling to return. Will it extend to employers who do not employ people on their race because they are seen as more likely to take sick leave? Reports indicate that 'people of colour were 54% more likely to be fined than white people.' Further investigation is needed to determine evidence of unlawful and actionable race discrimination by the police.

Disabled people face similar workplace problems, but with the added complexity of the duty to make reasonable adjustments. Issues arise from the lack or removal of social care services and new legislation that has suspended rights to some council services.

Parents (especially women) with childcare responsibilities have also been disproportionately affected. According to a survey by Pregnant Then Screwed 78 per cent of mothers found it challenging to manage

Analysis by University College London has found BAME people are two or three times more likely to die from COVID-19 than the general population.

childcare and paid work during lockdown. As a result, 57 per cent thought increased childcare responsibilities had either negatively affected their career prospects or would harm them in future. A further 25 per cent said their employer had not been flexible enough to allow them to complete their work duties while providing childcare. And, as schools and nurseries began to reopen, almost half said they felt forced to send their children back so they could focus on work. This is born out in our own enquiries.

It is not just women, as some men (though many fewer), have had to shoulder childcare. It raises the issue of whether being a parent or even just those parents with school age, or younger, children should also be a protected.

Professor Joan Costa-Font of London School of Economics said 'Not only pandemics such as COVID-19 affect older people harder, but its policy reactions have revealed the lower social value of older populations, which explains why many have died alone or in isolation amidst delayed lockdowns. The underfunded system of long-term care services has turned nursing homes into "death homes". And when faced with the need of critical health care, they have been given a lower priority.'

There is already a public law case against the Secretary of State for Health and Social Care regarding care home victims. It is possible that similar claims may be brought in the county court for age discrimination as well as a combination of more than one protected class, race and disability; or age and disability; pregnancy and race.

The Equality Act 2010 s14 contains a provision that covers more than one ground of direct discrimination – known as combined or dual discrimination. The government deemed it too 'complicated and burdensome' for businesses so did not bring it into force. Perhaps now is the time – although its scope is limited as it fails to cover harassment as well as indirect discrimination.

The issues are wide ranging and fast moving. Given the current Government's direction of travel, with coded references to reducing the burden on business and the reintroduction of employment tribunal fees, it is unlikely we will see any great strides to strengthen discrimination law by legislation. All the more reason therefore why lawyers must use existing available tools to fight against discrimination.

Audrey Ludwig is director of legal services at Suffolk Law Centre.

Lynn Vernon | Behind closed doors

When the pandemic hit and lockdown began social workers were no longer visiting families face to face. Contact centres were closed. Everything seemed to stop.

Except, of course, things did not stop – or at least not in terms of what was going on behind closed doors. We have yet to see the full extent of how many children may have suffered harm. What we do know is that many more children have become vulnerable during this period.

As a childcare solicitor/advocate I meet families on a daily basis who rely on support services to keep the threat of care proceedings at bay. At the same time society relies on agencies such as nurseries, school, doctors and Child and Adolescent Mental Health Services (CAMHS) to alert us to children who may be suffering harm. We take this for granted. It was suddenly horrifying to think that there was nobody monitoring the most vulnerable children in our society, who were at home 24/7 with parents, who struggle at the best of times without the additional pressures of lockdown. The sad reality is that most of the time we can only help those who seek out our help or those who are already known to be in crisis or need. We know that there are some families that fall through the cracks – lockdown made those cracks seem wider.

Lawyers can be guilty sometimes of taking the court process for granted. We can often forget the impact on clients experiencing court for the first time. The alienating nature of the process for parents has never been more apparent as it was during lockdown. We have glibly expected clients to dial in, listen, not speak and 'behave'. Hearings at court can sometimes seem like they are just about the lawyers, with parents as bit-part players. However, telephone hearings where judges can mute parents (as one did when a parent dared to start voicing their unhappiness at events) simply take away the voice of clients. It has been our job to ensure this doesn't happen. We have had to adapt taking instructions virtually using the telephone/Facetime/WhatsApp. We have had to listen more carefully and remember that clients need the chance to tell their stories and feel that they are heard.

If we continue with remote hearings post the pandemic then we lose all the benefits of face to face hearings – the chance for parents to see the social worker and guardian at court and vice versa; the chance for grievances to be aired, the chance for us to actually take instructions from a client who struggles to engage at other times.

As lockdown started to ease, I attended a three-day 'hybrid' final hearing in person with all parties present, save for a witness who attended by Zoom. There were definite improvements to the usual court experience. It was well organised with only two courts open on each

Now we must remember to listen and ensure that families are heard. Most of all we need to redouble our efforts to put families at the very heart of the care system.

floor. Meeting rooms were guaranteed for all of us – no taking instructions from a distressed client in the corridor for once! Listing didn't slip in any other hearings, meaning we had the judge's undivided attention for the whole time. It felt like the parents were being treated in a more respectful way and that their case held more importance, rather than just one shoehorned in amongst many others. But of course, it only worked because resources were made available – not something we can often rely upon.

Perhaps COVID-19 and its impact has provided an opportunity for us to reflect on how we manage the court process for families. We can do much more to ensure that the court experience is more inclusive and much less alienating for those we represent.

As we reflect on the pandemic and the consequent lockdown, rather than focusing on the ways we have had to adapt our practice to cope, we need to think about how we do the things that we do. We have needed to find new ways to communicate, new ways to take instructions. Now we must remember to listen and ensure that families are heard. Most of all we need to redouble our efforts to put families at the very heart of the care system.

Lynn Vernon is a solicitor and director of Covent Garden Family Law.

Cris McCurley | Working with the women's sector to combat domestic abuse

There have been so many unexpected challenges and positives of working in this area during these crazy times. I need to begin with a massive thank you and shout out to all of our IDVAs, ISVAs, refuge workers and everyone working in the domestic abuse sector, particularly those in the specialist BAME organisations who have faced the biggest risk and challenges. They are an unsung and overlooked yet essential part of our emergency services, protecting us and saving lives: and boy have they been in demand.

That these specialist services have continued to exist against all odds following over a decade of savage funding cuts, has been heroic, and they have continued meeting the ever-increasing demand for services through the pandemic, *and* without PPE.

During lockdown we have seen an unprecedented escalation of domestic abuse (as well as an upsurge in domestic homicide) with those impacted cut off from family, friends and support, and isolated with their children behind closed doors with the abuser. It was a huge set back when the Ministry of Justice (MoJ) refused our call for legal aid to be available for protective orders on a non-means-tested basis. We were only asking for this to be at legal aid rates, and only during the period of lockdown, and in spite of being told many times by civil servants we discussed it with that it was a reasonable ask, and one that would save lives, ultimately the response was an unbelievable no. Instead Government advice was about how victims can apply online for DIY protection – thankfully this was quickly withdrawn when it was pointed out that this advice could place them at greater risk as they would have to make the application under the eye of their abuser.

I can't remember a busier period for family practitioners in my working life. There have been so many positives including the court's promise to prioritise urgent applications for protection. Against that is the challenge that, after months of discussion with the MoJ and Legal Aid Agency (LAA), many women and kids still cannot access legal help because we still have a legal aid means test which deems them to have available capital to spend on legal fees when it is tied up in a property that they own jointly with their abuser, and to which they have no access. It is shameful that we still have to turn women away who desperately need legal protection but cannot get it, or in the alternative, see them go into debt they cannot afford in order to get the orders that they need to safeguard themselves and their children.

I can now say that I am starting to see the beginnings of hope, for a new era of appropriately identifying and addressing domestic abuse across the whole of the justice system, in a way that will have a trauma-based approach, and will properly work to safeguard and save lives.

Having remote hearings has always been something I have been instinctively against, but I have had to say they have had unexpected and welcome benefits. As a practitioner, I have been able to be far more productive in my working day: If I have a remote hearing at 10 am, I can be working until the phone goes, put my jacket on, and I'm in court. Most hearings have been positive experiences, especially for the client who isn't having to commute to court, worry about seeing their opponent and his mates staring at them across small waiting area that they have to share, or sit next to them in the court itself. Many have told me how much better that feels and I hope that for short hearings, we can continue to run them this way. I accept contested hearings are a different matter, but the time saved has meant that those of us doing this work have had more time to spend with the increased number of referrals, which has been a blessing.

Also not twiddling their thumbs during lockdown have been those of us working on the development and amending of the Domestic Abuse Bill, which is starting to look like something that we want it to be.

Lastly, a final shout out and massive thanks to members of the Family Private Law Courts and Domestic Abuse Inquiry panel who have worked their socks off to get their final report out in time for its many and much needed recommendations to impact on the final draft of the Domestic Abuse Bill. I can now say that I am starting to see the beginnings of hope, for a new era of appropriately identifying and addressing domestic abuse across the whole of the justice system, in a way that will have a trauma-based approach, and will properly work to safeguard and save lives. The inquiry report is something that I read with great joy as a rallying call for positive, much needed change: There is obviously still a lot of work to be done . . . but BRING IT ON!!!

Cris McCurley is a partner at Ben Hoare Bell LLP.

Michael Etienne | Exclusions in the new normal: an irresistible demand for change

The government's whiteboard now has the '1 September 2020' as the date on which all schools will re-open for all pupils across the UK. During lockdown, pupils and parents have had to contend with reductions in the State's duties to meet both care and educational needs, cancelled exams and uncertainty about when and how schools will re-open. However, (another) prospective date for the re-opening school gates needs to come with at least two more things. First, a pledge to keep more pupils in their classrooms by committing to an immediate and tangible reduction in the use of exclusions in the new term. Second, and necessarily, a willingness to confront the systemic discrimination that persists in our education system.

The latest annual figures for school exclusions, published by the Office of National Statistics on 31 July 2020, paint a frustratingly familiar picture. It is one that has added significance because those who are most at risk of exclusion are also from groups hardest hit by all aspects of the pandemic. They include disproportionate rates of exclusion of children with special educational needs and disabilities (SEND), those on free school meals and those who have been in care. Twenty years on from The Macpherson Report and with the latest demand that Black Lives Matter having only just been remade, pupils from Black Caribbean backgrounds and those of mixed heritage are still three times more likely to be permanently excluded than their white peers.

Behind that are Black pupils, boys especially, criticised and often penalised for being 'aggressive' in ways that other pupils would be more affectionately described as 'boisterous'; 'chatterboxes' that are more likely to be described as 'loud' and 'disruptive' if they are Black girls. More pernicious still is the policing of appearance and expression: pupils excluded for having an Afro, for dreadlocks consistent with Rastafarianism. Others may face the prospect of two-hour detentions for 'kissing their teeth' – something that would surely provoke an outcry for what would be neutrally described as tutting.

The detrimental impact of school exclusion on pupils, their families, but also society more widely is so well-established that it would be trite, were it not so serious. Excluded pupils, particularly the permanently excluded ones, are less likely to complete formal education, or to do so with grades below their peers, vulnerable to criminal exploitation and over-represented in the criminal justice system.

The detrimental impact of school exclusion on pupils, their families, but also society more widely is so well-established that it would be trite, were it not so serious.

The Serious Case Review into the murder of Jaden Moodie that concluded in May 2020 was another reminder of a well-known truth. At 14 years old, Jaden was brutally murdered in a dispute over drugs. He is now recognised as one of the youngest victims of county lines drug-dealing. In its review, London Borough of Waltham Forest found that he had spent all but three of the last 22 months of his life out of education, having had a history of exclusion. The review went on to emphasise that time out of education, for whatever reason, can increase a child's vulnerability to criminal exploitation. Like so many of the headlines that have come and gone in the last few months, we knew this already.

There are three features that connect not only the exclusion cases I defend but also the experiences of many of my prison law clients: historically undiagnosed SEN, other unmet needs, manifesting in persistently challenging behaviour. The unmet need that features often is in mental health support. The government's guidance to schools about the mental health impact of COVID-19 on pupils says all the right things: that children may be returning to school after a bereavement, a family breakdown and facing nuanced mental health difficulties as a result. However, the school exclusion guidance already requires consideration of all of a child's circumstances, it warns that persistent misbehaviour may be a sign of unmet need and emphasises the importance of early intervention. That has not reduced exclusion rates for pupils with SEND. The pandemic alone will not right that wrong.

Against even this relatively short background, there are two unavoidable conclusions that governors, their head teachers and politicians must now confront head-on. The first was reached by the Institute for Public Policy Research in 2017 (among others before and since):

'[O]ur education system is profoundly ill-equipped to break a cycle of disadvantage for these young people.'

The second, which is even more sobering 20 years on from the Macpherson Report, is that of the Runnymede Trust, in June 2020:

'Racism is deeply embedded in schooling . . . that schooling must be radically re-imagined to place a commitment to antiracism at its core.'

It is impossible to overstate the challenges facing children and young people, not only now but in the decades ahead. The pandemic will exacerbate all the worst effects of exclusion as it has done with so much else. Therefore, the imperative that school leaders – governors, their head teachers, as well as the Government – commit to keeping more children in their classrooms than ever before is irresistible. Almost all of the excluded pupils I have represented have been part of at least one disproportionately excluded group. Questions about the extent to which the disproportionalities have been specifically considered are often met with generic references to 'ethos' and purportedly robust equality and diversity policies. Those generalisations must now give way to specific and candid engagement with the systemic inequality that is an undeniable reality in even the best of schools.

On 27 May 2020, the Minister of State for School Standards, Nick Gibb, expressly declined to give an assurance – consistent with the Government's insistence that schools must reopen for the well-being of the most vulnerable pupils – that pupils would only be excluded in the most exceptional circumstances. After the relegation of the absolute duty to meet EHC Plans to one of 'reasonable endeavour'; the creation of 'easements' allowing local authorities to suspend compliance with their Care Act 2014 obligations; and the extension of the timescales that apply to the EHC Plan process and to reviews of school exclusions: the test for permanent exclusion was conspicuously untouched. Whenever schools re-open, there is one certainty: none of us can afford a return to business as usual.

Michael Etienne is a public law and human rights Barrister at No5 Chambers.

Kate Aubrey-Johnson | The youth justice system locks down

In March 2020, the emergency measures in response to COVID-19 confined children to their homes, closed schools and made it a criminal offence to meet with friends or hang out in the park.

Internationally there were calls for blanket protection of children from arrest and detention during the pandemic. The UN Committee on the Rights of the Children and the UN Office of the High Commissioner called for all children to be released from custody. Such protections were not introduced in the UK. In fact, no children left prison as a result of the COVID-19 early release provisions, and the government took no steps to release unconvicted or unsentenced children despite the harsh conditions in the secure estate.

The Coronavirus Regulations 2020 and the innumerable amendments placed the responsibility for adherence on the 'responsible adult'. So, largely, the concern that children would be arrested for breaching the regulations was not realised.

In circumstances where children's lives were transformed overnight, exams cancelled, future plans placed in limbo, the stability and structure of school, training and employment suddenly absent. There was a reasonable expectation that the youth justice system would shift focus, take a welfare-based approach, as it is legally obliged to do. What emerged was a chasm between the guidance which was progressive and child-rights centred and police actions on the ground. The Interview Protocol agreed between the CPS and the National Police Chiefs' Council sought to avoid any non-urgent arrests or interviews, but in practice this was routinely ignored.

Children continued to be arrested for low level offending, and such offending was more visible to police officers while most people were remaining in their homes. Being arrested became far more distressing for children, given the risk of contracting the COVID-19, as police officers did not wear PPE. Once detained at police stations, lawyers were no longer routinely attending in person and appropriate adults attended but wore PPE leaving children feeling yet more isolated and frightened.

The immense speed with which the justice system pivoted to a more virtual world meant that youth offending teams (YOTs) started to conduct assessments over video link. Lawyers provided police station legal advice over the phone. But this left children bewildered and with heightened levels of trauma, as they found themselves with no face to face interaction with adults to support them.

In fact, no children left prison as a result of the COVID-19 early release provisions, and the government took no steps to release unconvicted or unsentenced children despite the harsh conditions in the secure estate.

Initially many hearings took place online, with administrative hearings conducted with children participating in hearings virtually whether from their homes or the secure estate. The most recent study on the impact of remote hearings was published during the pandemic. It is a stark reminder that remote hearings are unsuitable for vulnerable defendants, particularly children. Defendants appearing over video link are more likely to be remanded in custody, more likely to receive custodial sentences and vulnerabilities and hidden disabilities are missed.

Even before the pandemic, delay hampered the youth justice system. Last year, children commonly waited four or five months for their cases to come to court, with delays of 12 to 18 months not uncommon for serious cases. The impact of delay is felt more heavily by children, it affects their ability to recall events and the fairness of the process. Children are going through a period of maturity and change, so the passage of several months means their lives have often moved on by the time their case comes to court. The adverse effect causes particular unfairness to children turning 18. So the delays and backlog in the justice system are extremely concerning for children's rights. In particular, when about a third of children in custody are on reman, of these, two-thirds will go on to receive a non-custodial sentence.

As the justice system looks to the future, it is hoped that COVID-19 may leave behind a positive legacy. In pre-COVID-19 times, there was always a presumption in favour of diversion for cases involving children, however this was not routinely the case. The CPS are undertaking a review of all cases and the CPS Coronavirus: Interim CPS Case Review Guidance encourages specific consideration of the impact of delay on cases with child defendants and to consider whether an out of court disposal may be appropriate. It is hoped one legacy of COVID-19 will be greater use of diversion, enabling children to receive informal out of court disposals and cautions without proceeding to court.

Other innovations may be that we will see the participation of professionals using video link. This could lead to a more collaborative approach by enabling input from children's services as well as other professionals such as educational psychologists and child and adolescent psychiatrists providing attending hearings remotely. It may also be that if Nightingale Courts are introduced, youth court cases will be heard in community settings more suited to enabling the effective participation of children.

There are some less positive impacts of COVID-19. There are whole cohorts of excluded children who have been left without any provision for education, training or employment and they are vulnerable to exploitation by county lines gangs so the rise in youth crime is a likely consequence. Policing during the pandemic appears to have entrenched the disproportionate treatment of BAME people – this is one of the biggest challenges facing youth justice. The huge backlog of trials and consequent long delays are likely to impact children more heavily. The youth courts resumed trials in March and are hearing cases with child defendants on bail and in custody and capacity continues to grow. For children in the Crown Court, however, there is an even bleaker outlook. Trials are being adjourned, some for over a year until September 2021. It is likely many of the children on remand awaiting trials in the Crown Court are in multi-handed trials where there is simply no prospect of listing these trials. It is also clear that there continues to be a push for virtual hearings, and specifically video remand hearings with suspects at the police station having their first court appearance on video link – any virtual hearing for child defendants raises alarm bells.

Kate Aubrey-Johnson is a barrister at Garden Court Chambers.

Jacqui Appleton | Ring, ring . . .

It's 00:11 hours and there it goes again. It hasn't stopped. My call log shows 42 calls today – the first of which was over 18 hours ago at 6am.

I've another 8 hours and 49 minutes to go before my 24 hour 'duty slot' ends and my day job begins.

I've got a pre-arranged voluntary interview at 0730 which I moved from 1000 because I'll be in court at that time and no one else is free to help. It's 50:50 whether I'll get any sleep at all between now and then.

Hello, It's the Defence Solicitor Call Centre (DSCC), we have a duty case for you at XXXXX Police Station if you can accept?

When someone is arrested the police call the DSCC to log the case, the DSCC call the solicitor to deploy the case, and the solicitor then calls the police to say they've accepted the case. It's a nonsense and complete waste of time and money, but there you have it.

I duly accept the case and 'ring in' . . . there's no answer, but I am obliged to keep calling and eventually the phone is picked up by the detention officer (DO) who is run ragged. DOs are the unsung heroes of the custody block. I have spoken to three separate shifts of custody staff today – the early shift, the late shift and now I'm on the phone to the night shift.

Defence solicitors are often 'on call' from Friday at 5pm through to Monday at 9am. We don't get paid to be on call and, while we may not be working the entire time, it is impossible to relax or do anything because the DSCC could ring at any given time. We work the weeks either side of our on call weekends, with nights on top of days, because this job is 24/7/365. We can't work shifts; there's simply not enough of us. The average age of a duty solicitor is 47. The government cuts and lack of work/life balance has led to a big drop in young lawyers entering criminal law.

I am exhausted and secretly hoping the DO will say the magic words I desperately want to hear 'it'll be a morning job.' Nope. *'The officer is ready to go, I'll get him to phone you.'*

We can't work shifts; there's simply not enough of us. The average age of a duty solicitor is 47. The government cuts and lack of work/life balance has led to a big drop in young lawyers entering criminal law.

I turn the big light on, splash my face with water, make a brew and open the biscuits. The officer phones and tells me the brief circumstances of the alleged offence that my client has been arrested for. I phone the DO back and he takes the phone down to my client's cell for us to have a private consultation. It cuts out – twice – because there's no signal in that block. The DO moves my client to an interview room where we can hear one another clearly.

Although I'm cream crackered, I tell myself that it 'could be worse' because, pre-COVID-19, I would be putting my coat and shoes on right now to embark on the dreaded 45-minute middle of the night drive to the station. I hate driving in the dark and, on no sleep, it's dangerous. How I feel right now, I wouldn't do it.

Upon speaking to my client, I have concerns about his fitness and make representations for him to be seen by the mental health team prior to interview. The calls ping pong back and forward for the next two hours and at gone 2am, it's decided my client will be 'bedded down' and assessed in the morning (the interview actually commenced over 12 hours later at 3:45pm in the afternoon).

Could I get back to sleep? No chance! The biscuits I'd needlessly scoffed to keep me awake for the interview meant I was now left there wide-eyed. I finally drifted off when the DSCC called again at 03:44, 03:46 and 04:51. Three more cases and more calls back and forth. The DO confirmed they would be 'morning jobs' (phew!).

My alarm went off at 06:30 – leaving me just enough time to sort the kids out and get ready for my 07:30 interview to be followed by the madness that is Monday morning remand court.

Jacqui Appleton is a partner at Shelly & Co Solicitors.

Melanie Simpson QC | Racial injustice in the criminal justice system

When Theresa May, an architect of the hostile environment that led to the Windrush scandal, said 'If you are black you are treated more harshly by the criminal justice system than if you are white', she was stating the obvious.

During the COVID-19 lockdown the police stopped and searched 30% (22,000 people) of London's young black men aged 15-24. Predictably 80% of these stops resulted in no further action. This targeting of a new generation of young black men creates a continuum of lost confidence and mistrust in the police, no different to that expressed in the decades old Scarman Report.

Racial injustice exists everywhere but it is highlighted in the criminal courts most acutely because liberty is at stake and they should be place of justice for all.

We have to expunge our criminal justice system of the demonisation of black men where in evidence age old tropes are used to demonise them in court. References to 'gang members' and 'knife-wielding youths' have taken over from 'black muggers' but race is still a central theme. White people are the overwhelming majority in this country and carry out the overwhelming number of crimes but the phrase 'white on white violence' does not exist.

In too many cases there is a conflation between the use of the word 'gang' and urban or black culture. We see evidence introduced seeking to prove that someone is in a gang just because they are in a street music video and look, dress and talk in a certain way; when some are only there because they live in the area and think that it's a cool thing to do. During one of my trials, I had to challenge a police gang 'expert' who gave evidence that the words 'a long ting' meant a long knife, when anyone in the black community knows that it means something taking a long time. I have heard officers give evidence that hand gestures made by black defendants in a photo are a gang symbol and I've had to put together a photographic collage of white dignitaries, including the Pope, doing the same gestures.

We have to expunge our criminal justice system of the demonisation of black men where in evidence age old tropes are used to demonise them in court.

The stereotyping of black youths being in gangs is highly racialised. The 2018 Amnesty UK report 'Trapped in the Matrix' found that there was a staggering 'conflation between gang members and urban culture'. The numbers speak for themselves: 78% of those on the gang matrix were black yet the number of black people responsible for serious youth violence was 27%. It is also worth noting that 40 % of people on the gang matrix had never been convicted of a serious or violent offence yet their inclusion becomes 'intelligence' which can be taken into account when a decision is being made in relation to bail.

Crown Court juries may very well be the saviour of the criminal justice system. Successive reviews have found that juries are the one place, in the criminal justice system, where there is no systemic racial bias. My experience as a trial advocate bears this out. As advocates we can strip away the prejudices and stereotypes so that the jury get to see the person whose fate they will decide. It is one of the reasons why black people in the UK seem to instinctively trust juries even when they have a general mistrust of other elements of the criminal justice system.

When a black person is convicted the bias returns. Black people are more likely to receive a custodial sentence and that sentence is likely to be higher than that of their white counterpart.

When the Lammy Review was carried out 41% of those aged under 18 in youth detention were from minority groups; in 2019 that figure stood at 51%. The latest figures on young people in detention show that the only two groups where the numbers have not reduced are for black and mixed-race youths. The figures also show the danger of using the term BAME as a catch all, because in the BAME category the number has gone down which reflects that fewer Asian and 'other' identified youths are placed in custody.

More diversity among judges will help to remedy some of the injustices. Only 1% of judges self-identify as black or black British. I know how important it is to have diversity – when we look at all the participants in the criminal justice system we need to see our society reflected at all levels.

There is no doubt that racial discrimination exists within the criminal justice system. The real question is why so many recommendations for legislative reform are still gathering dust. The answer to solving systemic injustices lies in implementing, at the very least, the recommendations contained in the Lammy report.

We have to acknowledge the role that anti-black racism plays in our society. These are complex problems rooted in historical events, political decisions and majority apathy to serious inequalities and harm.

The BLM movement has brought these issues to the fore and as people listen, learn and form greater allyships there are those of us who are watching out to see the signs of real change.

Melanie Simpson QC, 25 Bedford Row.

Rhona Friedman | The victims, not the recipients of justice

The lockdown in London was lived out in weeks of azure skies of startling clarity. In the absence of the usual filmy haze there was dread, stillness and quiet, the hum of the city replaced by the underlying pulse provided by the numbers of dead ticking upwards beyond accident or misfortune into the realms of world beating political incompetence. Then George Floyd was killed, and the streets burst into life with new voices making new demands many of them focusing on the justice system.

With the rest of social and economic life in stasis why the justice machine had to keep running albeit in a stripped down way and how the system reacted to the crisis illustrated both the casual disposability of the rule of law in neo liberalism and conversely the huge ideological and psychological investment in seeing that a coercive expression of the rule of law inheres.

After too many days in March in which the justice system appeared in a liminal state its borders patrolled by the Keep Calm and Carry On commissars, the senior judiciary and the magistracy belatedly gave in to the science and suspended almost all hearings. Most courts may have been closed for weeks but remarkably the rate of arrests in London hardly dipped. The thin blue line had to be seen to be holding. But who was being policed and why?

By 19 June 2020, 44,000 stop and searches had been carried out in London in May. This was the highest monthly rate since January 2012 and more than double the rate of the year before. Stop and searches carried out on black people increased 7.2 per 1000 in March to 13.5 per 1000 in May. An investigation by Liberty found that the new Health Protection Coronavirus Restrictions resulted in BAME people in England being 54% more likely to be fined under coronavirus rules than white people.

We saw through lockdown the hierarchies of carnivalesque behaviour. Suburban bunting and cake-fuelled white conga lines all fine, block party fun for young inner-city Black, Asian and white working-class people not fine. A cross country plague run from London N1 was found retrospectively to fall within permeable and elastic government guidance whilst a black man in Manchester running errands for his shielding mother was handcuffed and threatened with pepper spray.

Then came 25 May 2020. We now all know systemic inequalities are death-dealing and so when the 8 minutes 46 seconds ended and George Floyd was dead the Black Lives Matter Movement's demand for wholesale system change became something that makes reformist notions of improving the system and delivering fairer 'outcomes' look anaemic and ultimately self-serving, the status quo triangulating and resistant to self-examination like a politician's sorry not sorry.

There is a profound reluctance in the UK to acknowledge that too often black people are as Angela Davis identified many years ago 'the victims, not the recipients of justice.' However, critiques of a racialised justice system have become impossible to ignore. Disparities maintained by race, class and power are being interrogated in real time by people arming themselves with the intellectual armoury of Davis, Fred Hampton, Audre Lord and Ruth Wilson Gilmore.

And so when people dismiss defunding the police as nonsense in a way that suggests it is a notion so juvenile that it is not worthy of debate they say so from both a position of privilege but also with no appreciation of the history of decarceral critical thinking which began in the United States. There for decades academics and community activists have identified that the maintenance of structural inequalities comes about through over policing internally othered communities as part of the long game of excluding people of colour from the wealth and levers of power that colonialism and slavery created in the first place. It's a neat trick exposed and destabilised by what to some seems like the sudden arrival of calls for a diversion of funds away from prisons and police.

Now for the first time there is a broader awareness that what many thought were uniquely American ills; brutalising policing and racialised justice outcomes are home grown and endemic.

The US has the highest prison population per capita in the world but the review conducted by David Lammy MP in 2017 found that England and Wales imprisons a higher percentage of black people. In the same year as the review was published it became a crime not to give voice to your otherness by refusing to state your nationality audibly in court. The requirement was quietly withdrawn in July of this year but whilst it was in force every criminal lawyer will have heard someone identify as black British or white English. That response denotes an acute understanding

107

What became properly visible as a reaction to the pandemic was the machine teetering on the brink of a state of exception, the normal checks and balances of liberal democracy suspended as a reaction to crisis.

that the requirement was a further expression of racialised profiling linked to punishment.

The system is supposed to operate with inbuilt checks and balances but the problem inherent in a technocratic approach to fairness with no underlying change to structures of inequality is exemplified by codification of sentencing. The introduction of the Sentencing Guidelines has not achieved fairness unless fairness is measured by the metric of more people getting longer sentences.

What became properly visible as a reaction to the pandemic was the machine teetering on the brink of a state of exception, the normal checks and balances of liberal democracy suspended as a reaction to crisis. There were calls to reduce the number of jurors or abandon the use of juries entirely. This at a time of renewed examination of unequal outcomes when the jury system is one of the only features of the criminal justice system seen as a leveller and corrective to the racism which pervades the rest of the system.

The pandemic has resulted in the suspension of rights on one hand and the performative rule of lawism on the other with extended sitting times and the creation of pop-up courts to tackle a backlog caused by years of under investment and over prosecution.

The main lesson from the pandemic is that the carceral state is impelled to continue with its economies of harm; surveillance, stop and search, handcuffing and arrest whilst legal protections have been shredded by access to justice cuts, court closures and the undermining of fair trial rights. But the demand for change in the justice system and beyond is impossible to ignore and attempts to dilute it or technocratically manage it away will result in a corrosive crisis of legitimacy.

Rhona Friedman is a criminal defence solicitor and co-founder of Justice Alliance.

Patricia Daley and Queenie Djan | The Black Lives Matter Protests

Black Protest Legal Support UK ('BPLS') serves as an independent hub of Black and Brown lawyers that have come together to provide free legal support to UK Black Lives Matter ('BLM') activists and protesters. The organisation was founded by Ife Thompson, whose primary aim was to monitor policing at BLM protests and assist those impacted. In accord with our founders' vision, BPLS is coordinated by Black and Brown Lawyers, with a keen interest in countering the impact of structural racism on black individuals.

Legal observing plays an important role at any protest, in ensuring there are independent people attending, gathering evidence, advising activists of their rights and effectively 'policing the police'.

BPLS coordinators have been on the ground with 125 volunteer legal observers since the very first large London protests on the 3, 6, and 7 June 2020, monitoring and documenting evidence regarding police behaviour. These first protests were to set the tone for upcoming protests and bring about distressing questions and conclusions as to the tactics deployed by police and the emerging pattern of behaviour towards largely Black and Brown protesters and our legal observers.

It is a shared sentiment amongst our Black and Brown legal observers, that their experiences during the protests across London, predictably reflected the same concerns about police brutality that sparked both these protests and the broader Black Lives Matter movement in the first place.

From the very start of the 3 June 2020 protest, during a team briefing regarding health and safety, police officers standing nearby taunted and mocked our volunteers marking remarks such as 'Are you here to ensure social distancing or just to cause trouble?', 'Do you really think you have any powers because of hi vis jackets?', 'You're on the wrong side?', which made Black and Brown legal observers worry what was to come for them and for protesters.

Throughout all three days of the June protests in central London, we witnessed police physically and verbally intimidating peaceful protesters. Specifically, on Westminster Bridge on 7 June 2020, where it was reported by a group of our legal observers that officers manhandled a pregnant woman and dragged her across the police cordon. Legal observers also noted one officer using excessive force to pull a man off his bike, then proceed to drag him along the ground away from the crowd.

Our Black and Brown legal observers were repeatedly threatened for noting officers' publicly visible badge numbers. On one occasion one of our legal observers was injured after being aggressively pushed by the police. On 11 July 2020 a legal observer was subjected to verbal transphobic abuse by officers while carrying out their duties at a protest in Hackney. Unsurprisingly for us, our white legal observers reported a more positive experience during their interaction with the police.

It is worth noting the stark difference in policing tactics during overwhelmingly white demonstrations such as Extinction Rebellion. Though, it is not necessary to

The criminalisation of predominantly young Black and Brown people exercising their right to peacefully protest is alarming.

go that far back to compare. The 13 June 2020 BLM protest erupted into chaos when the English Defence League interrupted a peaceful protest. The interaction between predominately white groups and police was a far cry from the policing at previous BLM protest. The police were subject to openly aggressive behaviour but did not respond with kettling in excess of four hours or using 'personal information' as bargaining chips for people's liberty.

From what we have seen on the ground peaceful protesters at BLM demonstrations were subjected to police brutality. We felt a growing concern for young people, including vulnerable children, who were kettled by the police. There was a disregard of the police's duty to safeguard and protect them even during a pandemic. The criminalisation of predominantly young Black and Brown people exercising their right to peacefully protest is alarming. It is a known fact that, black children are already disproportionately policed and that BAME children are overrepresented in the youth justice system, accounting for over 50 per cent of the young people in detention. The police becoming enraged when dealing with young black people protesting or legally observing which we believe is connected to the expressions of bias and stereotyping towards young black people demonstrated through their policing tactics such as 'stop and search'. Twenty years since the Macpherson report, and the Metropolitan Police Service is still struggling to deal with institutional racism. The issue with the force is structural, you can have a very well-meaning officer, who still supports racist structures, even if their own beliefs aren't overtly racist.

Black Protest Legal Support encourages any protesters impacted by these and other issues to contact us, so we can provide appropriate legal support.

We will continue working to monitor police behaviour at these and future Black Lives Matter protests, to ensure those attending are safe and supported.

Patricia Daley and Queenie Djan are members of Black Protest Legal Support.

Lydia Dagostino and Jane Cleasby | Protests, policing and the pandemic

The policing of protests during the pandemic has been a cause for serious concern, both now and as it continues beyond the summer. The myriad of regulations are changing constantly, with law enforcement struggling to keep up with what they can and can't do. With social distancing likely to continue in some form or another for the foreseeable future, peaceful protest is under threat.

In May, we advised and assisted people who were arrested for participating in a gathering of more than two people, at an Extinction Rebellion (XR) protest in central London. They maintained social distancing but were still arrested.

Those who are unfortunate enough to be arrested during the pandemic will be taken to police stations were the level of compliance with social distancing measures is varied. In some parts of the country, the police are complying, but in others there a very few safety measures in place.

On 24 April 2020 (a month into lockdown) the CPS and police, following nationwide pressure from defence lawyers, agreed a protocol for police station interviews stating that wherever possible advice and assistance should be by telephone and video link. The success with which this has been implemented is again varied and seems to depend on the availability of the technology and the inclination of the police. On the plus side, it may be now possible to get advice from the solicitor of your choice even if they are on the other side of the country.

In the courts, things are simultaneously static and chaotic. Many of those arrested during the XR October Rebellion in October 2019 still haven't had their first appearances to enter a plea. Hearings remain stubbornly listed and then are often adjourned at the last minute. Many people have been required to physically attend court to answer charges despite the risk posed by COVID-19, or risk warrants being issued or even being convicted in their absence. Some have pleaded guilty by post, for convenience.

The police approach to the Black Lives Matter (BLM) protests has been variable. In London, mounted police confronted BLM protestors outside

Downing Street on 6 June 2020. In Brighton, the police have kept a relatively low profile during BLM protests. In Bristol, when the Edward Colston Statue was pulled down on 7 June, the police did not intervene, and it was several weeks before they published images of those they were seeking and even longer before they started making arrests.

No doubt, their investigations have been hampered by the fact that the vast majority of those present wore face coverings as protection from COVID-19. (It's worth noting that a study released by the National Bureau of Economic Research found that BLM protests had no measurable impact on the spread of COVID-19.)

Under Section 60AA of the Criminal Justice and Public Order Act 1994, in certain circumstances the police have the power to require you to remove a face covering. One might expect that during the pandemic the police would refrain from using such powers. However, during BLM protests in London on 7 June, legal observers reported that police were requiring protestors remove their masks so they could be filmed, as a condition of being released from a kettle.

A week later, the Chair of the Police Federation of England and Wales urged the Home Secretary to be to take the draconian measure of banning protests whilst the virus posed a threat.

With the summer in full swing and the prospect of an economic nosedive, those who have lost faith in the democratic process may see protest as their only chance to have a voice.

With the summer in full swing and the prospect of an economic nosedive, those who have lost faith in the democratic process may see protest as their only chance to have a voice. Although social distancing measures have been relaxed, current regulations still prohibit gatherings of more than 30 people. While that is the case, the police can be expected to continue to treat measures meant to protect public health as more tools in their public order arsenal.

Lydia Dagostino is director of, and Jane Cleasby is a paralegal at, Kellys Solicitors, Brighton.

Deborah Coles | The culture of immunity and impunity

The murder of George Floyd, the brutal dehumanisation of a black man restrained to death was shocking. However, for many black and indigenous communities across the globe this extreme manifestation of state violence and racism was all too familiar. Deaths in custody and state violence are a global human rights issue.

The Black Lives Matter protests have provided a reminder that this was, and remains, a systemic problem in the UK set within the broader context of empire, slavery and colonialism. These diverse protests have also provided renewed impetus for debates about police accountability, defunding and demilitarising the police and prison system. This debate is all the more urgent at a time when exceptional police powers are being used to harass and criminalise black communities, the government and prison authorities have imposed mass solitary confinement as a response to the pandemic rather than release prisoners and intend to build more prisons. And when despite all of the heightened risks to detainees, immigration powers continue to be used to detain people.

The issues raised by the death of George Floyd are not new to INQUEST. For decades we have documented how a disproportionate number of black people die after the use of lethal force and neglect by the state. These are not isolated tragedies, but part of a systemic problem. They represent a pattern of cases synonymous with state violence, structural racism and injustice. Black people are at the sharp end of a continuum of over policing, criminalisation and imprisonment and cases we have worked on show in brutal reality what happens when institutional racism, racial stereotyping and racial profiling seep into the mind-set and into police culture and practice, that equates communities of colour with 'dangerousness' and 'criminality'.

We live in a culture of immunity and impunity in which state agents are rarely, if ever, held to account. Speaking ill of the dead has been a shocking feature of many state responses. Instead of acknowledging failures, we see attempts to demonise the character of the deceased as the 'drug addict' the 'gangster,' the 'mentally ill'. Time and again we see reference to the 'superhuman' strength of black men who have died struggling to breathe as they are restrained by police officers. The failings of mental health services and police responses have put black men at risk of double discrimination as seen by the deaths of black men in mental health crisis. The question this then begs is not about reform of police training and intervention.

We live in a culture of immunity and impunity in which state agents are rarely, if ever, held to account.

It is about why we are not funding culturally sensitive mental health services.

This is about also confronting the consequences of how race, gender, class, sexuality and disability intersect to place people at even greater disadvantage. Black women who have died in prison as a result of neglect, disbelieved, their disturbed behaviour treated as discipline and control problems, a situation also reflected on the outside when black women have experienced the violence of the state and died. Other issues include: the racial and health inequalities that has seen the devastation of COVID-19 deaths in Black and Asian communities; the impact of the hostile environment on so many Black people of the Windrush generation wrongly detained, deported and denied legal rights; the unjustified, often unlawful indefinite immigration detention system the preventable and forewarned fire in Grenfell Tower that saw the deaths of 72 men, women and children; the impact of race and class and the pursuit of profit over safety; the premature deaths of learning disabled people languishing in locked institutions; and the deaths of sick and disabled people waiting for welfare benefits.

Families have become powerful advocates and activists for change, turning their grief into resistance and galvanising action against injustice. Their struggles and campaigns provide a counterweight to state secrecy and a lack of formal accountability and have played a critical role in challenging the inequality, racism, discrimination and unacceptable practices of the state.

Time and again, after state-inflicted deaths and a plethora of recommendations from investigations, inquests, inquiries and reviews, promises are made by the authorities responsible, that lesson-learning, accountability and action will follow. For the families, every new death gives the lie to this promise and causes new pain. It is for this reason that INQUEST has called for the creation of a national oversight mechanism that will monitor deaths in custody *and* the implementation of official recommendations arising from post-death investigations.

Whilst enhanced accountability is important, what families tell us over and again is that they want action and change to prevent the same thing happening to another family. This is about radical, transformative change and a social justice agenda that rethinks how we address societal harms and prioritises meeting people's needs rather than relying on punishment and prisons. Providing welfare, health and social care in the community is the only truly humane and sustainable response to dealing with social problems, as the abject failure of the current criminal justice system, as illustrated by the revolving door nature of the prison population, has evidenced. Many of those who die in custody have been lamentably failed by other state agencies before their entry into the criminal justice system. Rather than expand the remit and resourcing of policing, the focus should be on investment in services that focus on reducing harm. A reallocation of criminal justice resources to well-funded, well-staffed community services, involving drug, alcohol and mental health services, youth services, jobs, affordable housing, schools and refuges should be the priority of the state rather than a return to the 'old' normal after the pandemic is over.

The energy of recent protests has enabled more conversations about how to create a safer, fairer and more equal society, thinking about prison abolition as a way of doing something radically different. As a result of our evidence-based knowledge and experience we have asked more challenging questions: why prison is used to address what are social problems of mental ill health, addictions, drugs, homelessness, poverty and inequality; why there is always a prison place but not a refuge space for a woman with mental ill health and a story of domestic violence and trauma; why there is always funding for more police weaponry such as the rollout of tasers but youth clubs are shutting due to lack of funding?

It is this evidence that INQUEST has utilised to adopt an abolitionist perspective to frame policy demands. In response to deaths in custody we have demanded an immediate halt to the prison building programme, and the diversion of those involved with the criminal justice system away from prison to community alternatives.

116

INQUEST is proud to be part of a social movement that calls for radical structural change. We owe it to those men, women and children who have had their lives cut short or have been harmed as a result of institutionalised state violence and been traumatised by the lack of remorse shown by state agents towards the dead and their families.

Deborah Coles is the director of INQUEST.

Dr Laura Janes | Prison law in lockdown

On 24 March 2020, the prison service went into lockdown.

Some 80,000 men, women and children in prison found themselves either in prolonged solitary confinement or in overcrowded conditions.

Prison is supposed to be a deprivation of liberty. That should be the limit of the punishment imposed. The rules that govern life in prison require that people in prison are supported to be able to return to the community safely.

This has been impossible during lockdown. Prisons became devoid of purposeful activity. Children in prison have had no face to face education, rates of self-harm in women's prisons increased and the entire prison population was starved of contact with the outside world.

Access to justice is always difficult for people in prison: they cannot look up their rights online or visit a lawyer. But during the pandemic it has been significantly worse. Problems have increased as prisoners have been deprived of basic rights, parole hearings cancelled and trials delayed without any indication of when they will be rescheduled. New and complex COVID-19 temporary release schemes were issued but legal aid was not provided to navigate them. All visits were cancelled and the availability of calls or video conferences with clients in prison is patchy.

Prison is a uniquely coercive environment. External scrutiny is key. Yet the shutdown of the prison system meant the exclusion of external visitors that usually check in with prisoners and report concerns.

At the Howard League where we represent children and young adults in prison, we have had to adapt our service, including moving to a remote service and putting our confidential helpline on a rota system. We managed to do this without any break in our service. We have been busier than ever: in the three months from 24 March 2020 we received around 2000 calls and spent over 4,500 minutes on the advice line. The intensity of the work has been immense. We have dealt with too many cases of children in solitary confinement for years – but during lockdown every young person we have supported is in solitary confinement. It's heartbreaking.

Working remotely means that incidental collegiate support is absent. Remote contact and supervision between colleagues is essential but not sufficient to compensate for the care and attention that comes from being together in the office. On top of that, everyone is dealing with unprecedented personal situations and they are inevitably affected by the horrors unfolding in the wider world.

We have dealt with too many cases of children in solitary confinement for years – but during lockdown every young person we have supported is in solitary confinement. It's heartbreaking.

This is the situation for lawyers who have been lucky enough to be able to continue working: many prison lawyers are based in criminal firms that have been sorely affected by the pandemic as court and police work has slowed. Many have been furloughed, which causes huge problems for unrepresented clients. Our access to justice service, through which we refer and signpost people to other lawyers if we cannot help, has become harder to deliver.

Perhaps hardest of all is the sense of sheer struggle and exhaustion that permeates the entire sector. There are the curt emails from exasperated professionals trying to function in a broken system that has been further incapacitated without warning: the social worker who tells you at 8pm on a Monday night that he cannot accommodate a child client granted bail on Friday because there are shortages due to COVID-19 and he will just have to stay unlawfully detained in prison; or a healthcare worker's snappy email suggesting your young autistic client should make his own representations if he wants to see a nurse after he has been restrained.

Yet despite all this so many lawyers have continued championing the rights of people in prison, adapting to new ways of working, some of which have been a long time coming. There has been an increase in the use of video platforms for conferencing; a greater use of telephone services for mental health in-reach, advocates and members of the Independent Monitoring Board; the ability of the prison service to increase phone credit; and the Legal Aid Agency accepting electronic files for billing and taking a more flexible approach to some things.

We must maintain the few positives that have emerged during the pandemic and build a more robust provider base that can withstand disaster.

Dr Laura Janes is the legal director of Howard League for Penal Reform and chair of Legal Action Group.

Charlotte Henry | Waiting on the outside: prisoners in the pandemic

In 2014 my brother Alex Henry was convicted of murder by joint enterprise. He was then 21. By the time we entered lockdown he had already served seven years of a 19-year minimum tariff and has been at HMP Whitemoor for almost six years.

My brother's guilt or innocence shouldn't factor when we discuss his treatment in prison. It should not matter that his family and many supporters say he is innocent and that the fatal blow was struck by another, but this distinction seems a requirement, when calls for the better treatment of prisoners habitually fall on deaf ears and we are forced to justify our concerns.

As the reality of an impending lockdown dawned, a helplessness took hold of my family which was above and beyond that usually felt by families of serving prisoners. By the middle of March 2020, our visits to Alex had been cancelled.

The prison population was predicted to be severely hit by COVID-19 and had been described as the 'perfect petri dish' for viruses due to the overcrowded and unsanitary conditions. Prison officers are not restricted to a single wing, but rather they travel through the prison estate freely without PPE to protect themselves or their charges.

To guard against protection Alex was issued 15 antibacterial wipes. Once they ran out he was unable to purchase any more. I reconciled with the belief that Alex was more likely to catch COVID-19 than I. I also concluded that, if Alex caught COVID-19, he was likely to suffer more compared to someone in the general population. The prison diet is deficient in both nutrients and calories leading to compromised immune systems. It has also been shown that a lack of sunlight, which produces vitamin D, can have a direct effect on the ability to fight off respiratory infections such as COVID-19. Alex countered this by purchasing a vitamin D supplement and extra food with the money we sent in. But this was also restricted as the amount of money he is allowed to spend is capped at £25 per week, and the items available to purchase by prisoners are inflated in price.

To guard against protection Alex was issued 15 antibacterial wipes. Once they ran out he was unable to purchase any more.

I worried that if Alex became severely sick, would he be taken to a hospital? The BMA conceded that difficult decisions may have to be made concluding that 'prioritisation policies' would include refusal of 'potentially life-saving treatment where someone else is expected to benefit more from the available treatment'. The term 'benefit' here is restricted to purely clinical considerations rather than the value attributed to their life. Despite this, I found myself wondering where would Alex factor if the equation became a 'moral' one, what is the value of a healthy young murderer?

In early April 2020, Alex hadn't contacted me for two days. This was when my nightmares began; vivid and terrifying. When Alex next telephoned me I could hear he had a cough. The following day he didn't call me. I dreamt that I travelled to HMP Whitemoor and the surrounding hospitals, but the prison did not let me in and I could not find him.

When Alex finally made contact again seven days later and reassured us that he was safe, the relief was unquantifiable. He told us he was now allowed 30 minutes out of his cell each day for a shower and either a phone call or exercise. However, with this freedom came the increased risk of infection, as he was forced to shower with other prisoners in a shared stall and the communal phone was not sanitised by staff between use. He said that a prisoner and several officers were suspected of having contracted COVID-19 and although they were now isolated, they had all associated with many others on the wing.

As the weeks turned into months, Alex's freedom grew marginally from 30 minutes outside his single occupancy cell to one hour. This de facto solitary confinement, has been shown to have serious mental health implications on prisoners causing increased anxiety, depressive episodes, anger, cognitive disturbances, perceptive distortions, paranoia, psychosis, self-harm and suicide. I noticed a marked effect on Alex's mental health when we spoke on the phone. He became irate, anxious and depressed. HMP Whitemoor allowed family members to send in DVDs, CDs and books, but it was the lack of daily human contact which affected him the most.

I relayed my concerns to our MP James Murray who I thankfully had an open dialogue with and in turn he wrote to the Ministry of Justice. He highlighted the distress caused by the lack of direct communication between serving prisoners and their family members and requested that access to in-cell landlines or mobile telephones be provided, to facilitate contact. I received a response from the Minister of State for Justice, Lucy Frazer QC MP, which although empathetic in tone, offered no solution and merely confirmed that the current restrictions were necessary. Frazer concluded that mobile telephones had been provided to 55 prisons, but because of the security risk, Long Term High Risk Security Estates (such as HMP Whitemoor) remained excluded from this scheme.

It is now July 2020 and as lockdown gradually eases in the community, this change is not mirrored in the prison regime at HMP Whitemoor. Alex continues to be confined to his cell for 23 hours per day, suffering severe social isolation, eased only by a single 10-minute phone call. However, HMP Whitemoor have finally facilitated virtual visits and we are told that socially distant prison visits may start in August 2020.

It is only when the crisis is behind us and the final tally on body and mind is taken that we will understand the impact on prisoners of the toxic combination of COVID-19 and Government indifference. I fear that in locking down prisons rather than adopting mass release as other countries have done the cure may have been worse than the disease.

Charlotte Henry is a trainee lawyer and the founder of JENGbA.

Toufique Hossain | Unable to breathe, locked down and locked in

We've been forced to spend endless days confined by walls. For the first time, deprived to some extent of our liberty. We could do nothing, it seemed. Just wait and hope it would change. That some good news might come. Some lost hope. Time collapsed in on itself. The days became indistinguishable; it became pointless counting or noticing, so we stopped. Liberty felt more precious than it ever did. It is in fact much worse for so many, living at the margins of society.

There is now, possibly, a pathway to empathy for what it might feel like to be caught in the vast net thrown over asylum-seekers and those locked up in the immigration detention estate.

There was no quiet period for us. The work began almost immediately after the government belatedly began to take the pandemic seriously. Dehumanising and longstanding government policies became acute. We took up the cause, at scale, of those held in immigration detention. It led to the single largest release of immigration detainees from detention. That did not immunise us from judicial criticism. Such is the intermittent fate of any claimant lawyer in this field. But things have changed, with extraordinary numbers of detainees obtaining bail, Courts accepting now that the unevidenced optimism of government, here deployed to detain and deport, has no basis.

We've had to do a great deal amongst ourselves to maintain collective and individual well-being. We've all had to contend with anxieties and loss in one form or another. No one has been far from pain. But the humanity and solidarity in my young team has only intensified. We as lawyers have had to evolve. We've had to carry on but with limited human interaction, to ensure clients are ok but without the face to face contact that can offer so much more assurance. Their voice is at the heart of our work. That has become even more challenging in an era of pixelated remote hearings. Our clients are resilient. But whether it's a mother and her children trying to stay out of horrific NASS accommodation or a detainee, with no prospect of removal being refused release even when at high risk to COVID-19 or due to the government's derisory level of support to asylum-seekers, a father being unable afford to buy nappies and food for his little baby; the pandemic has exposed the cruelty of the hostile environment.

Chaos is also being wreaked when it comes to accessing justice. Amendments to the Civil Legal Aid Regulations were steam-rolled in bringing with them more confusion and anxiety in preparing complex protection appeals. This has added yet another obstacle to ensuring justice for our clients. The lack of proper consultation in the name of 'emergency' has created another potential disaster that looms large for asylum-seekers and their lawyers, and so we are tooling up for further litigation.

And then we come to George Floyd. The deadly, brazen nature of racism was given expression in the ambivalent face of a white racist American cop. Those of us who have been listening to the endless suffering of people of colour here in the United Kingdom, know full well how the structurally racist policies of successive governments have suffocated migrants and their children for decades.

Malcolm X once said:

> 'A hundred years ago they used to put on a white sheet and use a bloodhound . . . Today they have taken off the white sheet and put on police uniforms. They've traded in the bloodhounds for police dogs, and they're still doing the same thing.'

Those enforcing the border and wearing its uniform are just as destructive. We live in a world of 'Go Home' vans, Brook House abuse, violent removals, the detention of torture survivors, Windrush, Grenfell, Jimmy Mbenga and Prince Fosu. The list is endless.

We're getting used to muting our laptops but it's time we unmute our voices and speak up.

As lawyers we can and should be positive. We have shown that through the law, change can come. Brave clients will stand up. COVID-19 has shone the light on those who still live in the shadows of our society, unable to breath, locked down and locked in. We're getting used to muting our laptops but it's time we unmute our voices and speak up.

Toufique Hossain is solicitor and director at Duncan Lewis, Harrow.

Jon Robins and Matt Foot | Pandemic or not, we need to talk about miscarriages of justice

Nothing like a pandemic to expose the frailties of our 'broken' criminal justice system to the harsh light of scrutiny. Not that readers need COVID-19 to remind them of the shortcomings of our courts. That's said, beware those with a vested interest – say, politicians or senior members of the judiciary – turning a crisis into an opportunity (eg pushing remote justice, limiting trial by jury etc).

Let's be mindful of deep embedded structural problems getting pushed to the back of the agenda. In short, it's time we talked about miscarriages of justice. All too often there is a cognitive dissonance at play in the debate over criminal justice reform. Everyone signs up to the notion that it is 'broken' but there is never quite enough time to discuss one inevitable consequence: wrongful convictions.

The tiny constituency of concern that has built around the issue which used to be front page news back in the 'bad old days' (Birmingham Six, Guildford Four etc) is finally making some headway. Two powerful podcasts have been broadcast. Ceri Jackson's excellent *Shreds: Murder in the Dock* tells the appalling story of the five men falsely imprisoned for the murder of Lynette White in Cardiff in 1988, and the painful process to get released. Mark Williams-Thomas's, *The Detective* concerns a current case known as the Three Musketeers, and the extraordinary circumstances they were said to have been involved in terrorism.

Widespread concern on the treatment of miscarriage cases generally led the All-Party Parliamentary Group on Miscarriages of Justice to institute a Westminster Commission into the Criminal Cases Review Commission (CCRC). Such momentum as has been built, can't be lost now.

The most cash-strapped part of our austerity/ pandemic-ravaged criminal justice system is its safety net. The CCRC's budget last year was £5.2m compared, down from £5.45m the previous year. When the miscarriage of justice watchdog opened its doors in 1997, its budget was £7.5m and it only had to deal with 800 new cases. Now it receives about 1,400 applications a year.

The Birmingham-based group has just one job to do. In her first public pronouncement, the current chair Helen Pitcher last year said that sending cases

Nothing like a pandemic to expose the frailties of our 'broken' criminal justice system to the harsh light of scrutiny.

back to the Court of Appeal was 'not be the be-all-and-end-all'.

We beg to differ.

As a watchdog, the CCRC could never be accused of being overly gung-ho. In its first 20 years, the commission sent 33 cases a year on average back to the appeal judges; however that number crashed three years ago when it sent a dozen cases back. Last year, just 13 cases were sent back and the year before 19 cases including eight concerning asylum-seekers convicted of entering the country with false documentation.

It is a bleak picture that is made all the more alarming by new revelations as to how the supposedly independent watchdog has allowed itself to be emasculated. At the time of writing a prisoner called Gary Warner is challenging the CCRC's decision to reject his case on the grounds that that it is not sufficiently free of Ministry of Justice (MoJ) control.

The independence of the commissioners (supposedly preserved by statute) is critical to the watchdog. It takes the agreement of three to send a case back to the Court of Appeal. From the start of the CCRC in 1997 until 2012, commissioners were employed on a full-time or near full-time basis on generous salaries (£93,796 in 2013) and a pension. Almost all commissioners are now employed on minimum one-day-a-week contracts and paid on a £358 daily rate which is significantly less than a basic judicial rate (for example, £502 a day for a judge in the First-tier Tribunal).

Thanks to Gary Warner's lawyers, we now know the change in terms and conditions was foisted upon the CCRC against the wishes of commissioners (all gone) and by a bullying MoJ seemingly suffering from collective amnesia as to why we needed an effective watchdog in the first place.

It's a dismal state of affairs: the CCRC has been treated dismissively by the Court of Appeal, starved of funding by successive governments for over a decade and finally neutered by its 'sponsor' department facilitated by its own weak leadership.

If the miscarriage of justice watchdog can't stand up to the bean-counters at the MoJ, what hope for the wrongly convicted?

If you are the victim of miscarriage of justice, the odds have never been more stacked against you. If by some miracle the CCRC refers your case to the Court of Appeal and its judges overturn your conviction (miracle #2), don't expect the state to compensate you for those hellish lost years. In the last two years, the MoJ hasn't paid out a penny as a result of the Coalition government's 2014 change in the law. Now to be eligible for compensation you have to be able to prove your innocence beyond reasonable doubt – in other words, our lawmakers have reversed the standard burden of proof.

It's a scandal. Pandemic or not, we need to talk about miscarriages.

Jon Robins is a freelance journalist. Matt Foot is a solicitor at Birnberg Peirce.

Rohini Teather | R is for Recovery

Three months ago, most of us were still going about our normal daily lives. Complaining about commutes, chatting with colleagues over coffee, doing school runs. Then lockdown occurred. Jobs were lost, salaries were cut while the self-employed and informal workers experienced catastrophic losses in income. The impacts have been worldwide and are likely to increase in the coming months. And far from affecting everyone equally, it is those poorest and the most vulnerable members of society that have suffered the most.

Every single reader of *Justice Matters* will know that the welfare system wasn't fit for purpose even prior to the pandemic. Over the past decade 'austerity' has been used as an excuse to hack away at social security entitlements, in particular for those living in poverty, the unemployed, people with disabilities and the sick. As an excuse to take so much money out of the legal aid system that lawyers are trying to help clients with their hands tied behind their backs. And as an excuse to slash and burn the courts estate and to keep legal aid rates the same for over twenty years.

So why am I hopeful that this the crisis may prove to be a national reboot in more ways than one? That under the guise of 'recovery' we may find a way of making the profession a more sustainable one?

Why do we need 'recovery', you might ask? The term is defined as a 'return to a normal state' be it of health, mind or strength. Some further 'R' words for you. Recruitment, Retention and Retirement. As I'm on a roll, I'll add in Reward. We know that there is a crisis in the legal aid system. We know that firms are finding it hard to attract new fee earners and to keep them. We know that the rates don't render this work financially viable, that advice deserts are blooming and that there are very real fears for the continued existence of the access to justice community. We know that there needs to be some fundamental changes made to return the system to its normal state and ensure that it is fit for purpose.

We hoped that some change may have come from the LASPO Review. It's probably fair to say that it came with more of a whimper than a bang and the general consensus was that it largely 'kicked

Every single reader of *Justice Matters* will know that the welfare system wasn't fit for purpose even prior to the pandemic.

the can' further down the road rather than addressing the multiple holes in the justice system. There were many, many consultations and meetings and ideas, but with the exception of the civil and criminal means test reviews, the LASPO Review did very little to address the fact that there are huge numbers of people unable to access legal advice let alone the issues underlying that. But I said that I was hopeful, didn't I? Here's why. Perhaps taking this post-pandemic period as point zero will make a difference. Right now, the government is putting financial measures in place to help a host of industries. Assisting in the recovery of the sector now, in the same way that other sectors are being rescued, may take some of the element of blame out of the equation. There is an opportunity now to make changes to the system not as the result of any perceived failures or mistakes, but rather as part of a more politically palatable 'recovery'.

As an All-Party Parliamentary Group for Legal Aid we will be focusing our efforts in the upcoming months on the shape of this recovery. We've formed the Westminster Commission on Legal Aid as a cross-party initiative to examine the state of the legal aid sector as it emerges from the COVID-19 pandemic. Over a period of six months commencing September 2020 the Commission will host public meetings to hear directly from practitioners across the civil, family and criminal defence spheres. The Commission will also gather and analyse quantitative data about financial viability and human resources from various strands of research. It aims to establish the current capacity of the sector to respond to client need, and to forecast how many organisations and practitioners will still be working in this area in three to five years' time.

Our intention is to demonstrate that now, as the country starts to shake off the crisis and to rebuild itself, is the time to invest in legal aid, to protect and future-proof the sector so that it can respond to legal need just as the nation needs it most.

Rohini Teather is Head of Parliamentary Affairs at Legal Aid Practitioners Group (LAPG)

Sue James | Out of the shop front

Betty has one kidney and a gastric ulcer. She is in chronic pain and says she can now only manage to eat sandwiches. She is 86. The stress of her case exacerbates her condition, but she can't get to the hospital for her treatment and the surveyor can't go in to report on the damage to her home – which is extensive. So, she has to wait. Her life on pause.

Betty sends long emails. Often. But she is the exception. With possession cases stayed, welfare benefit determinations on hold and our physical office closed, our usual clients have all but disappeared. They normally find us because something has happened – usually something bad: a possession summons, an eviction notice or a refusal of benefit. They find us when they are in crisis, often on possession days. But what if we could find them instead? And much earlier.

In Katherine, Australia, Dr Simon Quilty decided to trial a multi-disciplinary approach to treating his patients. He hoped to reduce the number of local emergency admissions because they were costly to both patient and hospital. The idea was to address the profound disadvantages suffered by Katherine's large Aboriginal population, including longstanding issues of homelessness and health and social inequalities.

Huge amounts of money were being spent on treating patients in the hospital, but when discharged patients returned to accommodation that would often have 30 people in three bedrooms, no air conditioning and thirty-degree heat. It made no sense.

Dr Quilty wanted to resolve the underlying drivers of hospitalisation such as homelessness or inadequate housing, so he invited a lawyer onto the team. Relationships were made with the other partners and trust was built with the patients. At the first team meeting, the lawyer identified 15 cases where legal action (or the threat of it) could make change for the patient. In the first year of the project, the findings showed a 50% reduction in emergency hospital admissions.

The law is often viewed through a criminal lens and so people with social welfare issues don't know they have a legal problem. Or one that can be resolved. They are much more likely to speak with their GP or their community about their poor housing, problems at work and family issues. The doctor treats the symptoms, but the causes of the problem remain unresolved.

When Peter Kandler set up the first law centre in 1970, he wanted to bring law to the people. Staff working in the law centre had to live in the area and be a part of the community. That is harder to do now but the idea behind it is still as important. As lawyers, we have to begin to take our services out from behind our shop fronts and into places where people are already seeking help. The health justice movement started with the most professional setting of trust – the doctors' surgery – but it could be anywhere. At Hammersmith Law Centre, we deliver advice in the Foodbank, sitting alongside people, building trust and resolving legal issues that have led clients into food poverty. Well, we were until lockdown.

Let's find our clients before they have to make the torturous route, across great deserts, to find us. Let's create a social justice network of lawyers, campaigners, community activists – all working together.

Ten years of austerity and punishing welfare reform have created the perfect storm. The pandemic hasn't helped. Structural inequality pervades our communities. With support services cut, there is no safety net and any statutory duties have to be hard fought. Lawyers are needed – we have the tools for change. Collaboration and co-location are key, but this means more than just being in the same place. It's about building relationships and trust within a multi-disciplinary team with a person-centred approach. To be successful, this change will involve a fundamental switch in how lawyers value their time and the financial investment to support it. But it has the potential to make lasting change.

We can't just sit in our offices anymore waiting for Betty to come in. The pandemic has pushed our services even more remote. Let's find our clients before they have to make the torturous route, across great deserts, to find us. Let's create a social justice network of lawyers, campaigners, community activists – all working together. Maybe then we can shake off the image of the wealthy privileged lawyer and reveal what we really are as legal aid lawyers – state funded public servants (without a pay rise for 24 years).

Sue James is a solicitor and director of Hammersmith and Fulham Law Centre.

Helen Mowatt | Lawyers must play their part and put themselves at the service of the movement for change

This series of essays has given an insight into the ways in which the pandemic and the Government's response has played out on the ground – in our justice and prison systems, at work, in the gatekeeping at housing and benefits offices, as well as of course in health and social care. The effects of COVID-19 have been felt everywhere by everyone, but the Government's handling of the virus has led to a number of life-threatening and, in many cases, fatal failures, which have had devastating consequences particularly for working class communities, those from BAME backgrounds, as well as disabled people and the elderly.

The experiences that have been outlined in these essays are not solely a natural consequence of COVID-19, but a product of political choices and serious failings in planning, preparation and implementation. There were failures in controlling the infection prior to and during its peak, as well as in its aftermath, for example in providing adequate PPE to those on the frontline, as well protecting care home residents and workers. There was a delay in providing ring-fenced funding to domestic abuse services, which led to women either remaining in abusive homes or being forced into homelessness – all during a time of heightened risk (a threefold increase into recorded killings) and a pre-existing lack of refuge provision. There were delays in advising disabled people who employ their own carers on keeping safe, and a withdrawal of safeguards for those who needed to shield. The failure to mitigate against the impact on those with disabilities, led to a disproportionate death rate for disabled people, especially for those under the age of 65.

BAME communities are up to twice as likely to die from the virus. As a result of structural racism and workplace discrimination, they are more likely to live in overcrowded homes, to have insecure, low-paid and frontline jobs, and are therefore more likely to contract COVID-19. The Government failed to mitigate against or even consider the disproportionate impact of the COVID-19 on these communities.

These essays have been written by lawyers, academics, an MP, members of civil society organisations as well as campaigners. But we all have something in common – we work with and on behalf of communities that have been the hardest hit by the pandemic and provide support and relief by assisting them with their most basic needs, such as food, shelter, and assisting with funerals. It falls on our sectors to pick up the pieces of the Government's failures, to support families affected by the crisis, and it is for that reason that we must demand answers.

We must encourage a creative, fearless and holistic approach to lawyering which whilst challenging the state through legal action, also recognises the limits of the legal system in enforcing real change.

That is why there have been calls for a properly resourced and rigorous public inquiry into the Government's handling of the pandemic, to hold officials to account and to prevent further deaths. The COVID-19 Bereaved Families for Justice Group (a group of over 1000 families) have campaigned extensively around this issue, and we (the Public Interest Law Centre) acting on behalf of the Law Centres Network and with the support of 80 organisations, wrote to the Prime Minister demanding that he not only commit to a full-scale inquiry in the future, but also ensure that an urgent phase of that inquiry is held now. Unless and until this happens, the Government will be unable to take the necessary steps to prevent further (and otherwise avoidable) loss of life.

But the Government's reaction to COVID-19 does not exist in a vacuum. A decade of austerity has pushed public services to their breaking point, and public-sector workers and their families into crisis. We should not be surprised that the Government prioritised the economy over peoples' lives. Cuts to our public services have meant that we were never in a position to properly respond to the pandemic. Our clients have borne the brunt of budgetary cuts in housing, welfare, health and social care. They have been worse affected by austerity and by COVID-19 due to existing health, economic and social inequalities, underpinned by a deeply embedded system of structural racism and discrimination.

We must encourage a creative, fearless and holistic approach to lawyering which whilst challenging the state through legal action, also recognises the limits of the legal system in enforcing real change. Such an approach seeks not only to transform systems and policies through advocacy and strategic litigation, but also, and crucially, to bridge the gap between lawyers, activists and frontline organisations. We must work together closely (both alongside and in addition to legal action) to build wider campaigns and social movements. Central to this approach is the development of strong dynamic campaigns that not only seek to reform systems and institutions, but ultimately aim for the social transformation of society itself – lawyers must play their part and put themselves at the service of that movement.

Helen Mowatt is a human rights and public law solicitor at the Public Interest Law Centre.

Carol Storer OBE | Undated

Do you hear that?

No. What?

That noise?

No. What noise?

It's like a howl?

A howl of pleasure? Or pain? Or anguish?

It's a low howl but it's getting louder.

I still can't hear it. Who is making the noise?

It's the people who are queueing up in food banks because they cannot feed themselves or their families.

It's the people who have insufficient money because the changes to disability benefits have left them unable to participate fully in life.

It's the people who never feel secure where they live because it is so easy to evict them. They cannot put down roots.

It's the people suffering violence from partners and ex-partners who cannot access meaningful help to protect themselves and their children.

Can you hear that noise?

Oh yes. That's been a low rumble for a long time. I tune it out. It's like living near a busy road. You learn not to hear the noise.

Don't you hear the noise is getting louder?

Since lockdown more and more people have learnt how difficult it is to claim universal credit and feed themselves and family members

Since lockdown more and more people have wondered if they will have a home in a few months' time.

Since lockdown more and more people have suffered violence in the home.

Since lockdown more and more people have lost loved ones, friends and colleagues and feel despair at the way that the pandemic has been handled.

Can you hear that noise?

Yes, it is getting very close.

That's everyone who has been warning governments about cutting services to the bone, that's low paid front line workers who have kept the country going, that's professionals who simply cannot take it any more saying they have had enough.

And can you see those people sitting by the side?

Yes, they look very dejected.

Those are legal aid lawyers who cannot take it anymore. They have worked 18-hour days, they have done more free work than paid work on many cases, they have been denigrated by the government, they are unsupported and at breaking point. They have given their all to their clients and to support the system. They do what they do to ensure justice for those who cannot afford to pay for it. But they are simply exhausted.

Will they keep going?

I do not know. I hope so.

Carol Storer OBE is interim director of Legal Action Group.